Curious Lancashire Walks

Curious Lancashire Walks

Forty intriguing country walks

by Graham Dugdale

First published in 2006
by Palatine Books,
Carnegie House,
Chatsworth Road
Lancaster LA1 4SL
www.palatinebooks.com

Reprinted 2008, 2010

British Library Cataloguing-in-Publication data
A catalogue record for this book is available from the British Library

ISBN 978-1-874181-33-0

Typeset by Carnegie Book Production
www.carnegiebookproduction.com
Printed and bound by Short Run Press, Exeter

Contents

Central Lancashire: Between the Lune and Ribble

South Lancashire: South of the Ribble

Introduction

'Not another walking guide to Lancashire!' If this was your initial reaction when perusing this book for the first time, then I urge you to think again and take a second peek. For this is no ordinary compilation. All the walks have at one time appeared as a regular weekly feature in the *Lancaster Guardian* under the umbrella heading of 'It's Great Outdoors'.

For the last eight years, I have been offering *Guardian* readers the opportunity to venture into the magnificent countryside that encompasses the North West of England. Although this particular volume concentrates on those in the country of Lancashire, the Lake District and Yorkshire Dales have also been popular destinations.

My intention has been twofold. The walks have all been personally compiled to provide an intriguing array of objectives for keen walkers to visit while enjoying a stimulating walk within easy reach of Lancaster. And by taking in a variety of unusual and enigmatic locales, it is also hoped that general readers will be encouraged to discover more about their local area.

With this view in mind, the current guidebook has emerged following numerous requests by readers for a compilation of these walks. Not that it is solely intended for readers of the *Lancaster Guardian*. Far from it. All the walks are self-contained encompassing a circular format. For those of a curious disposition who enjoy their own company and wish to delve into strange places, this is the book for you.

Be inspired by Jeremiah Horrocks, Lancashire's unsung hero from Much Hoole. Quake in fearful trepidation when seeking out the truth regarding the White Rabbit of Crank, not to mention the heinous murder perpetrated by Richard Pedder in Hambleton.

And then there are innumerable opportunities to explore the peculiarities associated with Lancashire's uniquely fascinating history. These range from the Roman occupation at Ribchester to the discovery of a Viking treasure hoard at Cuerdale; medieval field patterns near Yealand, to aspects of our industrial heritage at villages such as Dolphinholme and Calder Vale.

All walk routes correct at time of compilation; walkers are advised to use the relevant Ordnance Survey maps and to obey any local signage that indicates route alterations.

The Walks

Only a handful of the walks involve more than a modicum of upward perambulation, most being confined to the lesser heights in the western half of the county. Two of them venture onto the wild and desolate moorlands of the Bowland Fells, with one straddling the West Pennine Moors. Minor heights such as Ashurst, Billinge and Nicky Nook are little more than extended rambles. In consequence, none of the walks herein described should be beyond the capabilities of, dare I say it, the averagely fit walker.

The hand-drawn maps together with a lucid description of the route to be followed ought to be sufficient to enable participants to complete the walks successfully. Although it must be said that they can never be a substitute for the appropriate Ordnance Survey maps.

Public rights-of-way are made use of at all times and I have endeavoured to keep any necessary road walking down to a minimum. On my own maps, I make no apology for adhering to the imperial measure of feet. No bewitching connotation can be attached to 510 metres, this being the new height of Far Snape Fell and the highest point reached in this book. Far more exciting is the fact that you have climbed to 1,673 feet asl. Although it has to be admitted that metric distances have been used in the text. This is more as a concession to encourage younger readers to leave their ipods and computers at home to join their eminently sensible parents by using their feet for the purpose God intended.

If you enjoy these walks half as much as I did, then who can ask for anything more. And remember what the song says – '*Those boots were made for walking*'. So happy hiking and, let's go!

Pepper without salt

Monuments from contrasting epochs vie for attention amidst beautiful surroundings

Distance: 5 miles
Height: 250 feet (76 metres)

Start/finish: A free car park is provided at the southern edge of Eaves Wood on the road between Silverdale and Arnside

Terrain: Clear paths on limestone in the wooded areas are easy to follow

Shops etc.: Arnside

Explorer OL7 *English Lakes south east*

Prelude

The limestone country around Silverdale offers a unique environment that has been designated an Area of Outstanding Natural Beauty. 'Peppered' with rock scars and fluted carvings shaped by the constant trickle of ground water, the woodland trails are a joy to savour. Limestone chippings, also used for road surfacing, provide first class paths that are firm underfoot.

The woodlands in this area have been heavily 'coppiced' which is a system of tree regeneration that involves cutting back the tree growth close to the ground. Only broad-leaved trees are used, hazel being the dominant species in this area. This enables new shoots to come through at a much faster rate which was ideal for making charcoal in the days when it was required for iron smelting. The greatest expansion of coppicing took place in the eighteenth and nineteenth centuries when iron furnaces were in full blast.

Cutting down usually occurs about every fifteen years, after which the whole cycle begins again. It is important that the young shoots are protected from grazing animals who like nothing more than to nibble the tender shoots. Quite often the larger trees such as oak and ash are allowed to grow to full maturity giving the woodland a more balanced appearance.

The Walk

Set off by going through the stile at the top end of the car park. At the T-junction, head left along the lower edge of the wood. After a half-mile, take a right fork keeping watch for the storage tanks below left.

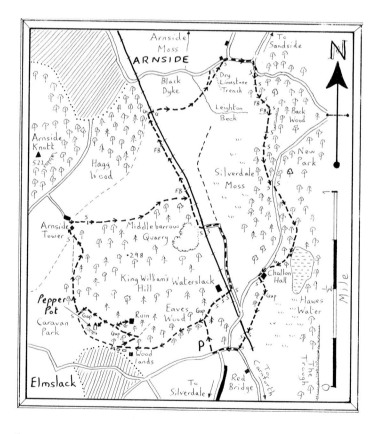

These were used as a water supply for the large house known as Woodlands which was once fed by springs. Home of the late Mr Dickens, it was he who donated all the land hereabouts to the National Trust on his death in 1949.

Take a sharp right up a gentle slope for 200 metres. Ignore the first path on the left but take the next obvious broad path. This eventually tapers into the rock stairway flanked by limestone guardians as a prominent wall is approached. Bear right up another flight of steps through a gate to reach the ruins of *The Gazebo*.

The gazebo was erected in 1830 to celebrate the accession of William IV who also gave his name to the hill on which it stands. Now hemmed in by conifers, only the foundations remain.

Retrace your steps back to the main path turning right through the wall gap and continuing onward beside a rampart of weathered scarring. Keep watch for a white arrow nailed to a tree pointing the way to the open plateau on the edge which resides the celebrated Pepperpot.

Circular with a conical roof, this endearing monument was initially suggested by the Hebden Family who owned the land in the late nineteenth century. Another proposal during the present Queen's Silver Jubilee year for an accompanying 'salt cellar' failed to materialise. Perched on the lip of an abrupt drop and

The landmark Pepperpot above Eaves Wood.

overlooking the modern housing development of Elmslack, this quaint yet well-loved edifice harks back to an age of gentility. A period when all manner of strange memorials appeared on the landscape to commemorate eminent personages.

Continue west along the escarpment through a loose scattering of trees for 100 metres before bearing right to rejoin the main path. Follow this to the crossfell wall that marks an end to National Trust property. Head left down through a wall gap to reach the lower path. Bend right here through a stile and along a path that skirts the upper edge of a large caravan park.

As the path makes a gradual decent amidst the trees, take a right fork to keep above the caravans which will eventually bring you into more open ground as a wall is neared. Bear left alongside the wall down to a stile at the bottom which adjoins Arnside Tower.

Gaunt and forbidding, this ruined stronghold once offered protection from marauding brigands. Known as pele towers, they appeared across England's northern landscape in the fourteenth and fifteenth centuries. They are stoutly built, usually three storeys high. The ground floor had no windows and was where cattle were herded. The main living quarters were on the middle floor with a private ladies bower above. Effective defence was provided by the flat roof, the whole building being linked by a spiral staircase. The tower at Arnside is unusual in being isolated. Most were incorporated into other buildings.

Continue down a clear track to the farm cutting right before the yard to re-enter Middlebarrow Wood by a stile. Accompany the woodland trail for a half-mile to arrive at a junction of paths close to the railway embankment. The route ahead leads to Middlebarrow Quarry. Our route swings sharp left to reach the edge of the wood. Cross a footbridge and head north alongside the embankment until you can pass beneath the railway beside an old signpost.

Accompany the concrete thoroughfare over the mossland and Leighton Beck until you are 50 metres from the entrance gate. Now fork right over pathless bumpy ground and over a stile to gain the Arnside road. Bear right past two left-hand road junctions for 300 metres until a stile is reached on the right. Enter the field heading south towards the edge

Arnside Tower – a relic from a bygone age.

of a small copse and another stile. Stroll down the walled corridor arcing left to a fence stile and footbridge.

Make the short crossing of a field to another stile and footbridge. Then walk alongside the wall on your right, the path being in a broad trench. Mount the wall stile at the end aiming for the next one ahead at the edge of a broad wooded tract here bounded by a fence. Joining a clear track which cuts through the wood, amble up to a road and cross straight over into the wood on the far side.

The track now makes a bee-line for a large expanse called Hawes Water as we enter the Natural Heritage reserve of Gait Barrows. Take the path on the right side of this reedy tarn which is famous hereabouts for the *char*. Climbing gradually, the path rejoins the road through a gate. Walk down the road for 100 metres turning left into the grounds of Challon Hall.

Straddle a stile at the rear and make a broad right hand loop down to a gap between two stone gateposts. Chaperone the fence on the left in a direct line to cross the railway track. At the far side, go along a short stretch of wall to gain the Silverdale road turning right back to the car park.

Back to the future

Ancient farming traditions rest easily within this Quaker community

Distance: 4 miles
Height: 350 feet (107 metres)

Start/finish: Park on the wide grass verge at Yealand Storrs where the broad limestone ridge levels off

Terrain: Easy walking on grass across a limestone ridge and drained peat mossland

Shops etc.: Yealand Redmayne Post Office

Explorer OL7 *English Lakes south east*

Prelude

Skirting the eastern flank of the Warton Crag limestone wedge lies the village of Yealand, or more precisely the twin villages. In times long since consigned to the history books, the landowner died leaving the land equally to his daughters; each share being named after their respective husbands of Conyers and Redmayne.

In keeping with this medieval tradition, the farming landscape in the area has likewise been preserved in the form of long strip fields common at a time well before the land was enclosed. Like many outlying communities, religious practices associated with non-conformist ideals still flourish. The Friends' Meeting House is easily passed un-noticed, having the appearance of an old cottage. A visit to its extensive graveyard dispels this false assumption.

With interior panelling that is original, it dates from 1692 and is thought to be the oldest Quaker place of worship in the country. When the leader of the movement, George Fox, arrived in 1652, one cleric unwittingly threatened him with a pistol. Perhaps he inadvertently thought this stranger in black had come to break up what were in fact illegal gatherings.

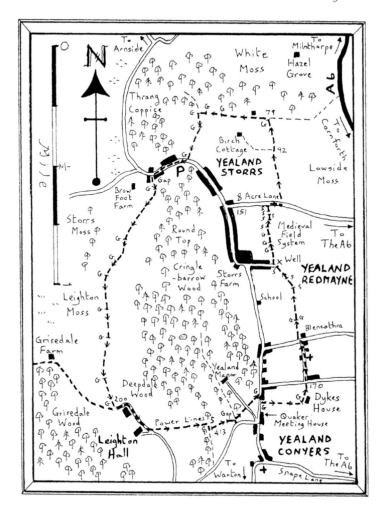

The Walk

From the tiny hamlet of Yealand Storrs, continue along the road towards Arnside until a narrow sign-posted wall gap points the way across the western flank of the Crag to Leighton Hall. At the end of the private driveway, pass through the first of eight gates that will eventually find you on the access road serving Grisedale Farm. This level track initially bends round to the right before heading south some 200 metres parallel with Cringlebarrow Wood on your left.

On reaching the road, bear left past Leighton Hall Farm and behind the Hall itself until you reach the front where the Park stretches away southward.

This grandiose Georgian residence was rebuilt in its present style by George Townley in 1763. Having no family the house passed into the hands of Alexander Worswick of Ellel Grange in 1805. He married Alice Gillow which began the famous association which continues to this day under the guardianship of Richard Gillow Reynolds. Leighton Hall has often been described as 'one of the most beautifully situated houses in England'. And who am I to disagree with such an acclamation?

Leave the paved drive to fork left up the rising grass bank accompanying a straight power line to the tree-fringed crest of the ridge. At the wall, bear right for 50 metres to locate a gate to cross an open glade dotted with limestone boulders. Wander across the grassy sward to a raised limestone plinth. Then drop down to a wall passing through a gap into the tree cover beyond. Bear half left down a path then through a stile and across open grass pasture. Go straight over the access road serving Yealand Manor to reach the gate that opens onto the road in Yealand Conyers. Head right for 50 metres then left through a gate strolling due east for a quarter mile keeping parallel to the hedge 50 metres over on your left.

On reaching Dykes House, go through the gate heading left along a track to cross over a village feeder lane. Walk along here past St John's Church with its squat tower to reach another lane. This is one of three churches in this tiny enclave which is a testament to the religious commitment that is generic within many rural communities.

Keep left of a large residence called 'Blencathra' to continue on a northerly course slightly offset to the left. At the end of a hedge passage, negotiate two gates continuing on the right side of the hedge. After the next stile, bear half left, soon mounting a fence stile

The Quaker Meeting House in Yealand Conyers.

to reach Well Lane and a fine old well restored by the Countryside Management.

It is perhaps 'well' to remember that this is how our ancestors obtained all their daily water supply. New housing has been erected right down the road to the well site which now appears a little out of place in this modern setting.

Continue down what was the old drovers' road along which cattle were moved to the population centres further south. The initial 200 metres are hedged on either side. A gate at the end marks the start of a spellbinding dip into the feudal system that flourished in 'Olde Englande'.

A series of narrow squeeze stiles, some gated, allow passage along the edge of the narrow strip fields. These were a furrow long, known as a furlong measuring 220 yards. This was the measure of one day's ploughing and was 25 yards wide. Some hedge boundaries have disappeared but are still clear to see. Each family would have been allocated a certain number of strips scattered throughout the parish, the best being reserved

13

for the more influential citizens. Operating a three-field rotation of barley, wheat and fallow, this medieval system of farming survived unchanged until the Enclosure Movement of the late eighteenth century. From that time, land was parcelled off creating the small fields more commonly associated with the countryside we now know and love.

At the end of this unique section, turn right along 19 Acre Lane for 100 metres before continuing north along the drove road. At its far end, pass through a gate turning immediately left past a smallholding.

This area is known as White Moss and became a lake following the last Ice Age. Reeds, trees and sedges eventually colonised the flats to form a raised peat bog. Drainage ditches keep the Moss from becoming too waterlogged.

After negotiating two gates, bear left off the main track through another gate to cross the adjacent field. Lean away from the wall to locate a gate at the far side. After passing through this, bear half right to reach the road at Yealand Storrs.

How Yealand residents once obtained their water.

Give thanks to Arkholme

History and a sense of pride mingle effortlessly beside the Lune

Distance: 5 miles
Height: 200 feet (61 metres)

Start/finish: Turn off the B6254 opposite the Bay Horse Inn and park down Arkholme's main street

Terrain: Gently rolling countryside encompassing hedged grazing for sheep and cattle

Shops etc.: Arkholme

Explorer OL7 *English Lakes south east*

Prelude

Many are the times that I have driven along the B6254 past the Bay Horse Hotel at Arkholme little realising that the road merely brushes the edge of the village. This secluded trait has to be Arkholme's chief attraction for those who live here. Quiet and unassuming, no other village is so well known yet remains one of the least visited.

Most people who claim to have visited Arkholme are unaware of the true extent of the village. The old settlement comprises a linear row of mainly seventeenth century stone houses straddling the narrow lane that slants down to the banks of the River Lune. Here on the raised site of an ancient Saxon fort stands a fourteenth century chapel dedicated to St John the Baptist. The bell measures 21 inches and is reckoned to be the oldest of its type in England.

Not so long ago, a ferry used to allow travellers to continue their journey along the right of way to Melling on the far shore. The ferryman lived in a cottage nearby. Originally granted a market charter in 1279, it was not until 1866 that Erwhum, as it was then known, became a parish.

Until that time, burials were conducted across the river valley at Melling, the funeral party having to make use of the ferry service.

15

One such cortege was swept downstream during a period of severe flooding and two people were drowned. What became of the coffin remains a mystery to this day.

At the end of this walk, a stroll down Arkholme's main street is heartily recommended. Many of the cottages have dates with the original owners initials carved into their door lintels. Unlike the modern off-comers on the opposite side of the main road, these were all individually designed and built. At the bottom, the street forks with one arm slanting down to the river and the other leading to the old church.

The saying used to be that 'Arkholme is on the sunny side but Melling is on the wealthy side'. A clear intimation that Arkholme was the poor relation, by not having its own consecrated burial ground. The chapel is located on the site of an old motte and bailey type castle similar to that adjoining St Wilfred's in Melling.

What makes the village of Arkholme truly remarkable is the fact that of the 59 men who marched off to fight in the trenches of the Great War, all returned safely; and this from a total population of 300. When you consider that towns such as Accrington recruited 'pals' brigades that were subsequently decimated in the fighting, this is an exceptional achievement. No wonder it is often referred to as 'The Thankful Village'.

The Walk

Our walk begins where a footpath sign points the way along a narrow passage which bears right at the end. A stile gives onto the field behind. Keep ahead across open grassland to reach a stile at the far left-hand corner. Now on the main road, head right towards the village past the Methodist chapel. Watch for the second footpath on the far side.

Heading west, cross a stile to stroll along a hedge soon passing through a gap. Keep to the fence on your left passing through a gate at the field end. Aim for the right edge of a line of trees to cross a footbridge and stile. Keep in a straight line nudging trees on your right to straddle a fence stile. Now head half right up a gentle slope to another stile on the crest of a broad dome. Bear left down to a wall

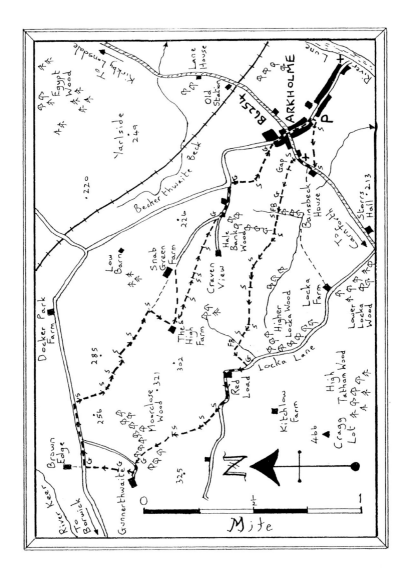

stile in a trough. Following two more wall stiles, cross a footbridge to mount a slope arriving at a wall. Slant left along this to reach Locka Lane.

Take a right here past the old farmhouses of Red Load. Two hundred metres beyond, mount a wall stile on the right dropping down a long grassy field. Make a wide right hand sweep with a fence stile midway to reach a wall stile. Bear left here over a low rise and down to the far corner which is wooded and has a stream. Now take the paved access road serving Gunnerthwaite in the Keer Valley. Just before you reach the buildings, bear right along a hedge up to a gate. Cross the next field to reach a back lane opposite the entrance to Brown Edge.

Bear right for a quarter mile until a signpost is reached on the right. If you have the time, keep ahead for another half mile to visit Docker Park, a working farm open to the public. Otherwise mount the stile

Red Load is an eighteenth-century farm near Arkholme.

The Bay Horse was a coaching inn.

and head south east alongside the wall on your right straddling three others along the way, the last being a ladder which lies offset to the left of our accompanying wall.

There follows a brief climb mounting a fence stile midway to the crest of a grassy knoll. On the far side of a fence, head right towards The High Farm. Once on the access track, bear left for 10 yards before heading right into the adjoining field over a fence stile. Aim half left to reach another at the far side.

Cross the next field locating an offset stile hidden from view. This is soon followed by another. Keep heading in the same direction (ESE) to reach a wall stile. Then spur down a long field to the gate at the bottom to join the Snab Green road. Head right to its junction with the Docker road.

Now go through the gate on the right and mount a rise. Keep right of a prominent tree to locate a corner stile hidden in the hedge. Then it's a straight walk down on the right of the hedge to reach the road on the edge of Arkholme.

Only now are you entitled to enjoy some well-earned refreshment at the Bay Horse followed by a wander into history down Arkholme's main street.

A Kellet's eye view

Two for the price of one across North Lancashire's limestone girdle

WALK 4

Distance: 6 miles
Height: 400 feet (122 metres)

Start/finish: Ample parking space on Longmere Crescent in Crag Bank

Terrain: Rolling pastures rise up from the coast in a series of limestone knolls

Explorer 296 *Lancaster and Morecambe*,
and Explorer OL7 *English Lakes south east*

Shops etc.: Carnforth

Prelude

Very few walks can be enjoyed that do not involve some form of transport to reach the starting point. In my own case, this is certainly one of them, and a fine local circuit it proved to be. Taking in both the Kellets, it is particularly noticeable that the underlying rock structure has been amply exploited since people first settled in the area.

Limestone is one of the most useful rocks known to man. From road materials, through to the use of lime as a fertiliser, to its vital use in steel making and the chemical industry, the exploitation of this light grey substance has resulted in numerous huge holes appearing in the landscape. Quarrying has always been a major source of employment in North Lancashire and our locality has more than its fair share.

Throughout this walk, the current importance of limestone is difficult to ignore. It has to be acknowledged that the companies involved should be commended for concealing their activities behind screens of trees. Certainly the motorway link to Leaper's Wood Quarry was a welcome improvement preventing the movement of heavy trucks through Carnforth.

All this talk of heavy industry and quarrying should in no way put you off this walk. Limestone country offers a unique landscape where woodlands flourish. A lack of surface water also greatly assists with footpath maintenance. It is noticeable that the expansion of quarrying has led to the re-routing of certain paths as the insatiable appetite for limestone continues to devour the countryside. Clearly this is a change that requires constant monitoring to ensure the conflicting needs of industry and recreation are recognised.

The Walk

Join the Lancaster Canal at Crag Bank heading north past the marina and the very popular Canal Turn pub – no stopping yet, you've only just started! Leave the canal towpath to cross the second bridge bending left along a parallel track. This soon forks away from the canal. Where it enters private land, take the gate on the right alongside a fence up to a stile at the top end of a chewed-up field. Still heading due east, cross the next field to a hedge stile and then onward to the motorway. Turn south the reach Kellet Road bridge. Now turn inland for the road walk into Over Kellet.

> Every nook and cranny of this award-winning village has a story to tell. Indeed the name Over Kellet means 'higher hill spring', a particular apt description. The broad acreage of green is proudly maintained and kept well trimmed at all times. On the right stands Hall Garth, a Georgian residence built in 1820 to replaced a much older structure.

> Opposite Hall Garth is the post office which was a dame school in days gone by. Stroll along the narrow land behind. Quaker meeting were held in Friendly Cottage the garden of which contained a simple burial ground at the rear. The green itself has an ancient preaching cross opposite the war memorial. The bones of St Cuthbert rested here on their journey north prior to being interred at Durham Cathedral back in the ninth century. The parish church also bears his name.

Slant right up the first connecting lane past Friendly Cottage then right again past the Eagle's Head.

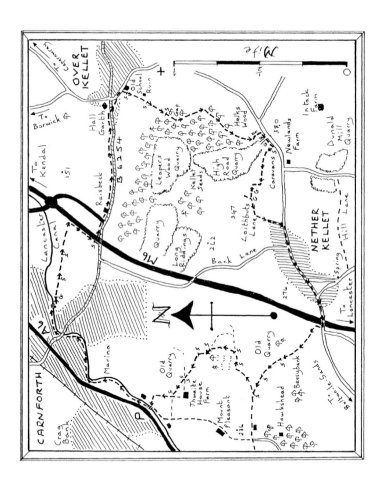

The ancient preaching cross on Over Kellet's village green.

Just up the road past the pub lies the old village school. Now a private residence, it was founded in 1677 as an endowed grammar school by Thomas Wilson. It had no playground so games were conducted on the road. New premises were built on the far side in 1973, which is just as well as Over Kellet lies on a busy crossroads.

Just before the old school, bear right up a flight of steps to reach the field behind. Continue ahead keeping right of a roofless barn to cross a ladder stile. With a hedge on your left, mount the facing slope to enter Slack's Wood close to Leaper's Wood Quarry. Numerous danger signs direct you away so keep left along a clear path to skirt the edge of Kit Bill Wood on the new section of path. This will eventually bring you to the edge of High Road Quarry.

Bear right past the entrance alongside a new fence, then right over a stile at the far side to follow a grass path up this side of the quarry planted with new trees. A thin path will eventually bring you to a fence gate followed soon after by another opening onto Laithbuts Lane. This is where the original right-of-way is rejoined. Head left along this old track down to rejoin High Road then bear right through Nether Kellet.

At one time there were forty lime kilns around Nether Kellet, so the Limeburners Arms is an apt name for what must be one of the most homely pubs in the country. Unlike all other pubs in the area, it exists in a time warp harking back to an age before plastic and hard sell.

Kellet is of medieval origin, and the name stems from the old Norse word Kelda, meaning spring. The village grew up around a particular spring that still exists at the southern exit on Shaw

Water still flows from Nether Kellet's original well.

Lane. All the villagers used to gather here for their water supply. Due to its purity and absence of chemicals, the water is said to be ideal for home brewing and wine.

Bear right immediately after crossing the motorway then left after 50 metres. Follow this hedged lane up to a stile. Continue over the hill and down to a hidden stile in the hedge. Bear half left over to a stile in the far corner to join a rough lane. Now head right and after mounting the second stile bend left in a wide loop along a grass causeway to reach a wall.

Mount the ladder stile accompanying the wall/fence round to another stile. Then make a diagonal crossing of the large field to reach a farm track stiled at each side. Bear half left aiming for a gate and gap stile at the far side thus avoiding Thwaite House Farmyard. Follow the hedged lane down to reach the canal bridge at Crag Bank.

A circuit around Carnforth

Your intrepid guide takes a nostalgic trip around his home town

Distance: 10 miles
Height: 400 feet (122 metres)

Start/finish: Turn off the A6 at Crag Bank down Longfield Drive. Over the railway, park beside the playing field at the bottom adjoining a sharp bend

Terrain: Hummocky fields enclosed by hedges with good paths for most of the way

Explorer 0L7 *English Lakes south east*

Shops etc.: Carnforth

Prelude

A circuit around one's own town or village using public rights-of-way as much as possible is often more difficult than you might suppose. This walk attempts to do this for Carnforth. It has the advantage of being relatively little used with no other walkers being encountered, and that on a glorious bank holiday weekend. A wide variety of man-made scenery was enjoyed together with an ever-changing pageant of rustic charm.

Our walk begins at Crag Bank. Gone are the smart tennis courts and croquet green from the 1920s. Today it has become merely a suburb of Carnforth with a host of modern housing developments effectively joining it to the mother town. The original stone cottages known as Dolly Tub Row which had large tubs for the collection of rainwater. During World War Two, the army began to use the area just beyond the playing field for target practice, an activity that continued long after the conflict had ceased.

The Walk

Continue down the shore road for a half-mile until a stile is reached on the right. Cross the field keeping to the right side to avoid any damp ground. Once over the stile at the far side, make a wide left-hand swing of this field then aim for the fence at the edge of the railway yards. Walk along the side to reach another stile at the start of a hedged track. This leads down to the shore road where a right will bring you to Warton Road.

Bear left under the railway bridge then over the River Keer. Turn right past Carlisle Terrace in Mill Head passing the football ground. At the end of the track, go through a stile followed by another after 200 metres accompanying a hedge all the way to a new housing development in Warton. Ahead the formidable bulwark of Warton Crag stands guard over this ancient settlement. **Be warned that after periods of prolonged rain, this section can become flooded and impassable**.

Remains of the Old Rectory in Warton.

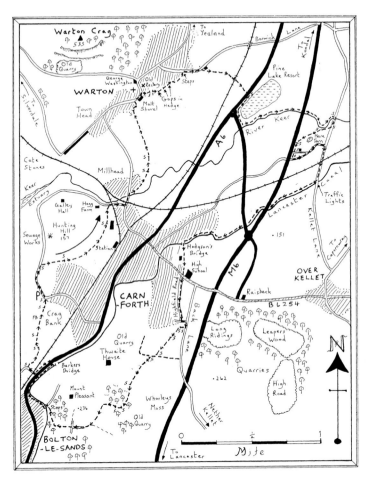

Gain the main street adjoining the Malt Shovel Inn, which was a popular coaching inn in the late eighteenth century on what used to be the main north-south route. Turn right through an archway just beyond the pub. Bear left behind the cottage and over a stile to cross a short field with another stile. Take note of the exposed skeleton of the Old Rectory on the left. Now maintained by English Heritage, it dates back to the fourteenth century and has a cruck-timbered frame. The thick stone walls afforded protection against marauding invaders from the north. Once it had ceased to be the local Court of Justice, this duty was performed in the Malt Shovel long before it dispensed alcoholic beverages.

Bear right alongside a hedge going through three gaps to pass behind a row of bungalows. Crossing a cul-de-sac, a narrow passage eventually brings us out onto a country lane up a short flight of steps. Head right for 200 metres forking right down a hedged track and under the railway to reach the A6. Cross straight over to mount a stile to head right around the outer boundary of Pine Lake Resort crossing the busy entrance by the roundabout with care until the River Keer is reached.

Head upstream under the motorway leaving the river at Kellet Lane. Cross the bridge taking to the fields on the far side of the river over a stile after 50 metres. Another follows soon after alongside the River Keer. After this bear half left over hummocky ground but keeping right of Hare Tarn and aiming towards the railway embankment. Follow this to pass through a farmyard crossing straight over the access road and onward to reach North Road.

Make a left along this road up to Kellet Road then right for a quarter mile to join the Lancaster Canal. Stroll back towards Carnforth until you reach Hodgson's Bridge – a distance that is a little over one mile. At the far side of the canal, walk up the paved passage between local schools, crossing over Kellet road and continuing ahead up Highfield Road. Bear left at the end to join the road to Nether Kellet. Head right for 50 metres only.

A stile in the hedge enables you to cross a narrow field stiled at its far side. Then bear half left up a rising bank beneath power lines. Keep in a direct line aiming for the midpoint of the hedge in front to mount the stile continuing onward heading south west to nudge a hedge corner. A straight line should find you straddling a hedge stile in the top corner of the field.

Bear right along a hedged farm track for a short distance only keeping a watch for the stile hidden on the left side. Maintain a south westerly

Carnforth Marina and the Canal Turn.

course to reach the far corner of this field to straddle the fence. From here keep left circling round the wooded marshland on your right along a grass causeway to enter a narrowing passage, follow this all the way to the crossroads near Mount Pleasant.

Go straight over into a constricted path hedged on either side. This leads round to the right through the woods of Thwaite Brow above the canal. Branch left off the path to descend some steps and over the bridge to join the canal towpath. Head back towards Carnforth leaving at the next bridge, walking back to the access road serving Detron Gate Farm. Wander down here then enter a hedged corridor on the right stiled at either end which leads out into drained farmland.

Head back towards Crag Bank beside the nearest dyke, mounting a stile midway along. Beyond a footbridge, bear half right to locate a hidden stile in the overgrown hedge. An enclosed corridor will then return you to the playing field.

Following the
Old North Road

Following in the footsteps of a celebrated pretender to the English throne

Distance: 3.5 miles

Height: 150 feet (49 metres)

Start/finish: Park on the grass verge at the crossroads
where Ancliffe Lane meets Bottomdale Road

Terrain: Rolling hedged pastures that undulate
in grassy waves

Explorer 296 *Lancaster and Morecambe*

Shops etc.: Slyne

Prelude

*In the twenty-first century, it is difficult to imagine that the main
road into Lancaster from the north was not always the A6. Indeed, in
historical terms, this road is a relatively new feature on the landscape.
Our walk today accompanies part of the older high road that parallels
the current highway a half mile to the east.*

*Known as Green Lane, it avoided what used to be marshland by
following a higher route all the way from Carnforth. Detouring slightly
through Bolton-le-Sands, its course was along Ancliffe Lane and so up
to the crossroads where we make our start.*

*Bottomdale Road is thought to have been of Roman origin and was
the main route taken by early monks based at Furness Abbey on the
far side of Morecambe Bay. They took the cross-bay route over the
sands arriving at Hest Bank thence striking inland. Their destination
was Halton to collect salmon from traps laid in the River Lune.*

The first Scottish army to march south along the Green Lane was

The manor house at Slyne where Bonnie Prince Charlie stayed.

that under the command of Robert the Bruce, who sacked Lancaster in 1322. Most notable however was the epic march south of Bonnie Prince Charlie in 1745 in an attempt to secure the English throne. Known as the Jacobite Rebellion it gained the support of sympathetic English dissidents along the way. Manchester in particular was a hotbed of ferment against the Hanoverian crown in the mid-eighteenth century.

Arriving at Derby, Charles realised the futility of his actions and turned back, retracing his steps and ultimate exile to France. The story of how the Young Pretender assumed the guise of a woman and was assisted by Flora MacDonald to escape the English has become the stuff of legends.

The Walk

Accompany the tramping feet of this army as it heads south along the Green Lane. The hedged track follows a relatively straight course soon passing a Transco Depot on the right.

There would have been no enclosed fields when the Young Pretender rode at the head of his invading force. In the

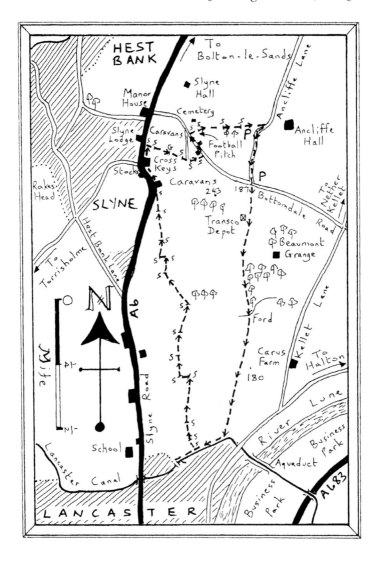

November of 1745, the going would have been tough along muddy and often impassable stretches of road. Between Lancaster and Preston, the road was reported as being an unusually good stretch.

After cresting the highest point the noble proportions of Lancaster Priory and the Castle would have come into view. Surrounded by the grey stone town below, it was a welcome halt for Charles and his supporters. He is known to have lodged with a Mrs Livesey at the Old Conservative House on Church Street on 25 November 1745, dining in a room at the rear. A blue Heritage memorial plaque commemorates this important event.

Today the scene is much changed. The priory is still there, but only visibile through the mesh of electricity lines. Other landmarks now take priority, such as the Ashton Memorial, Town Hall and Cathedral spire.

After crossing a ford, the track rises slightly before the descent to Beaumont where it runs alongside the canal, a late eighteenth century addition. After 200 metres, mount a stile on the right and follow the hedge along the right side of the field over two more stiles. Then bear away from a fence on the right striking up a shallow bank and aiming for an isolated piece of fence. Merge with a hedge on your left and follow it until a stile is reached. Climb over it followed by another after 20 metres to continue heading north. Our route follows the broad undulating ridge over three more stiles until a small copse of trees is reached.

Bear half left to cross the field diagonally to a stile at the far side then straight over the adjacent field. Here veer sharp left then right over two stiles passing into the next field. Slant downhill negotiating a hedged kissing gate continuing onward to join the A6 over a wooden stile at the southern limit of Slyne village. Although joined at the hip, the community known as Slyne with Hest is now regarded as the two separate entities of Hest Bank and Slyne.

Walk up the road passing the Cross Keys dating from 1727. Take particular note of the old stocks on the far side close to the aptly titled Hanging Green Meadow. A secluded rock garden behind is also worth a visit. Mount the hill continuing past a kissing gate located in a passage on the right. At the crest of the hill pause opposite Slyne Lodge. This is the first view travellers heading north have of Morecambe Bay and the Lakeland fells beyond. Just below is Manor Farm dating from 1681 where Charles Stuart paused for refreshment.

Return to the stile bearing left into the narrow passage with another stile at the end. Then mount a slight rise and down the far side through a gate and into a caravan park. Cross over the access road straddling a stile and leaning half left to the far side of the adjoining field emerging onto Bottomdale Road adjacent to a farm.

Bear left along the road for 300 metres then mount a stile on the opposite side to cross the football pitch, but only when no match is in progress. Otherwise go round the edge and through the stile on the far side into a small wooded dell stiled at each end. A short walk thereafter will bring you out onto Ancliffe Lane where a right will find you once again accompanying the old road back to the start.

Room for three in Slyne stocks.

A haven for twitchers

Ornithology and history mingle effortlessly around this western edge of Morecambe Bay

Distance: 3 miles
Height: Insignificant

Start/finish: The promenade car park at Bare adjoining the golf course and Happy Mount Park

Terrain: Clear paths all the way. Some care needed on the shore section due to tidal inundation

Explorer 296 *Lancaster and Morecambe*

Shops etc.: Bare

Prelude

Long before the railway station was built at Hest Bank, the village was well known due to it being situated at one end of the seven mile crossing of Morecambe Bay. Since time immemorial, travellers have chosen to reach the Cumbrian shore by this shorter though infinitely more hazardous route.

Unpredictable tides and quicksand are still a constant threat to those who venture out alone onto the sands of the Bay. The latest illustration of the extreme dangers posed were tragically brought to the fore when twenty-one cocklers lost their lives.

This is not only a recent phenomenon. Way back in 1325 following the drowning of sixteen people by the incoming tide, an official guide was appointed by the king. Being responsible for the safe conveyance of travellers and coaches, he was paid a yearly stipend of £15, a vast sum, which still holds to this day.

In the late eighteenth century, a coaching service operated three times a week between Lancaster and Ulverston being 'conducted by a sober and careful driver'. This ceased abruptly once the railway was opened through to Barrow. Apart from migrating flocks of birds, walkers are the only bay crossers these days. A one-way trip returning on the coastal railway is a popular summer activity.

These walks are invariably led by the renowned Cedric Robinson who has been a 'Queen's Guide' for over 35 years. In 1996 he received an honorary MSc from Lancaster University for unceasing efforts, not only as a guide but for preparing detailed reports on the shifting nature of the sands.

The Walk

From the car park, walk towards Morecambe turning left into Happy Mount Park.

First opened at Whitsuntide in 1927, its name stems from the rise on the left where the golf pavilion stands.

Turn off the main thoroughfare between the first buildings on the right to exit via a gate at the side. A wide unmade road bears left along the park fence narrowing after 200 metres. It is then a simple walk around the back of the park skirting some new housing on one side and the sprawling layout of the golf course on the other. We eventually arrive at the railway embankment veering sharp left over a footbridge and along the side of the track up to the crossing point.

Stiled at either side, the warning to STOP! LOOK! LISTEN! is sound advice that should be heeded at all times. Stroll across a short field and through another stile to pass beneath the main electrified line of the railway by means of a stone bridge.

Having passed beneath the bridge, swing left for 300 metres then right up a slight incline to reach the Lancaster Canal. A gap in the hedge opens onto the towing path where we head left under Bridge No. 116. Further along, a large selection of craft lie moored. The next mooring facility after this lies to the north at Carnforth.

Leave the canal bank just before bridge number 118 is reached and make a short detour over to the fine old hostelry that can be seen from the canal. This is known simply as The Hest Bank.

The projecting room facing the canal is called the old lantern turret and is where light was placed in the old days to guide

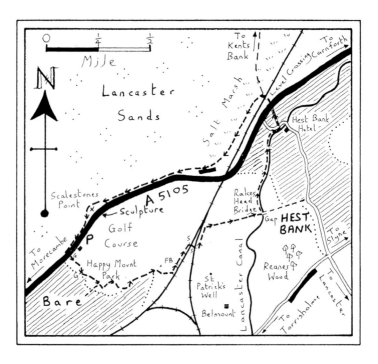

parties across the Bay during inclement weather. A hot meal and a bed for the night were doubtless welcomed wholeheartedly by weary travellers. Excellent meals can still be enjoyed at this most popular spot. First licensed in 1554, it was called the Sands Inn. In addition to the sale of such Elizabethan tinctures as mead, sack and honey beer, cockfights were held here each week. In the eighteenth century the inn became the haunt of rascally highwaymen.

The story is told of one brigand wearing a green coat who robbed a passing haulage wagon. Every man including the innkeeper who was found to be sporting a green coat was arrested and held in Lancaster Castle until the culprit could be identified. One footpad called Edmund Grosse was shot and

The Hest Bank Hotel – a welcome halt for cross-bay travellers since time immemorial.

wounded by the landlord in 1792. After being found guilty, the felon's body was gibbeted on Hanging Green for two years to deter other such poltroons.

Following an investigation of the pub and its attractions, re-cross the canal and head straight down Station Road. Cross over the main road and railway level crossing onto the shore. A grooved track made by stage coaches is still visible heading out across the sands to Grange on the far side. Our way lies left along the pebbled edge of the salt marsh.

Morecambe Bay is an important estuarine habitat for migrating birds who pause here for a refuelling stop on their journey between Canada and South Africa. Known as the 'East Atlantic Flyway', it is used twice a year by millions of birds such as the oystercatcher, curlew, dualin and redshank. Botanists also come to study the marsh flora such as thrift, sea aster, pearlwort and sea spurrey.

This accent on the natural history of the area has been taken up with gusto by the city council. Now well into the new millennium, Morecambe is making a positive effort to revamp its jaded image by emphasising this aspect of its attraction to visitors.

Continue along the shoreline past some houses and the Teal Bay Leisure Complex (now called VVV). Thereafter, a stroll along the promenade beside the breakwaters and rock armouring completes the walk.

Erected to combat flooding and the incessant hammering of the wall by the sea, they have been a resounding success. A recent addition to this part of the promenade is a splendid mosaic sculpture entitled Cupid and Venus *made by Shane Johnstone.*

Venus and Cupid overlooking Morecambe Bay on the promenade.

The plague challenged in Brookhouse

Aesthetic appreciation plus the healthy option
equal a happy populace

Distance: 4.5 miles
Height: 100 feet (30 metres)

Start/finish: Make use of the free car park next to the dual
bridges at the Crook o' Lune

Terrain: Easy going across enclosed meadows with barely a
hint of ascent, the walk encompasses the 3Rs
of rail, road and river

Outdoor leisure 41 *Forest of Bowland*

Shops etc.: Caton

Prelude

On a sunny afternoon, there can be few more delectable spots than
the entrancing Crook o' Lune. At this point the River Lune curls south
in a wide loop, almost meeting itself on the way back. The eminent
landscape artist, Turner, was so inspired by the view that he put the
arched span of the road bridge on canvas.

This was later paralleled by a railway bridge much used by holiday-
makers from the industrial heartland of West Yorkshire, a phenomenon
that gave Morecambe the nickname of Bradford-by-the-Sea.

The original Penny Bridge was replaced by the present structure
in 1883 after its central portion collapsed. Prior to this disaster, there
was no bridge at all and traffic had to ford the river. On the far side
of the road from the car park, there is the old toll cottage, which used
to exact the princely sum of one penny, allowing travellers to cross
the river by way of the aptly named Penny Bridge. Always open is the

snack bar for the end of the walk when a welcome cuppa will still be waiting. You haven't earned it yet, though!

The Walk

From the car park, descend the flight of steps to join the course of the old railway line now converted to a cycle/walkway. Head left across the rail bridge immediately upstream from Penny Bridge. Now on the opposite side of the river, take a leisurely stroll along the hedged track passing through two gates after a quarter mile. A little further along, the track bridges the access road serving Low Mill.

> *Once a noted textile factory owned by Thomas Hodgson, Low Mill employed many local people in addition to orphans brought over from the slums of Liverpool. Water for the steam-powered boiler was obtained from the adjacent millpond. Today the premises have been converted to high profile residences enjoying the finest of views across this beautiful sector of the Lune Valley.*

Stroll on past new housing development on the right until another link road is reached. Bear right past Caton's Catholic Church towards the main road heading left along here towards Hornby for a quarter mile. Cross the road and Artle Beck Bridge mounting the ladder stile to accompany the left side of the beck upstream. Beyond a hedge located midway, you will soon arrive at the road linking Caton with Brookhouse.

Swing left towards the latter for 200 metres bearing right up Hawthorn Drive into a modern housing estate. Leave it almost immediately up a narrow hedged passage with a stile at the end opening onto the field at the rear. Maintain a straight line to reach the opposite side of the field going through a stile and bearing left behind the houses.

When onward progress is barred by a fence, bend left through a stile and down a hedged corridor into a cul-de-sac. Over the road offset to the right is another passage that will return you to the Caton road. Bear right into Old Brookhouse, a total contrast and a millennium away from the modern part of the village recently vacated.

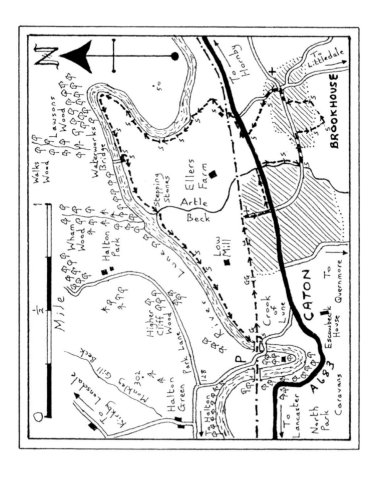

The stone bridge straddling Bull Beck adjacent to the inn is of particular interest. Built into the ancient parapet is the hollowed out Plague Stone dating back to the time of the Black Death in the late fourteenth century. This deadly disease wiped out much of the country's population having been passed on from infectious fleas carried by black rats.

To combat the epidemic, the residents of Brookhouse insisted that food traders deposit their wares on the bridge, the money being placed in the hollow filled with vinegar. It would appear to have had the desired effect of preventing cross-contamination, as fewer people died of the plague here than elsewhere.

Checking the Plague Stone in Brookhouse.

Turner's view at the Crook o' Lune.

Amble down the narrow winding Holme Lane opposite, forking left after 100 metres to mount a stile into the large field beyond. Head directly for Ellers Farm seen over the brow of the rising ground as you drop down to reach the main road via a stile. Bear right for 200 metres then slant left over the old railway and along a hedged field track to its termination.

Accompany this left bank of the River Lune in another wide sweeping meander up valley before a left wheel finds you heading back towards the Crook o' Lune. At the waterworks bridge, mount a stile then left around the structure to continue down river. Artle Beck is crossed by a set of strategically placed stepping stones after which the walk back to the bridge is straightforward.

Go under the old railway bridge veering left over a fence stile and up a grass concourse to reach the outward track through a gate. A simple left over the river will return you to the car park and that promised cuppa at the snack bar.

Key of the door at Middleton

An estuarine wander encounters magic and mystery alongside a maritime tradition

Distance: 4.5 miles
Height: 150 feet (46 metres)

Start/finish: Beyond the Old Rooftree Inn at Middleton, turn into Low Lane and park on the roadside

Terrain: Indistinct paths well stiled cross the fields followed by rough walking along the shore

Explorer 296 *Lancaster and Morecambe*

Shops etc.: Overton

Prelude

Until the Dissolution of the Monasteries under Henry VIII in the sixteenth century, Middleton parish was owned by the monks of Cockersands Abbey. The original manor house was replaced by the building now known as the Old Roof Tree Inn in 1440. It was later acquired by the Dalton Family of Lancaster after the monks had dispersed.

In those days buildings were often constructed around a 'cruck' framework – with huge timbers supporting both roof and walls – which is where the name stems from. These are still visible today and have helped to make the inn a unique edifice in the locality.

Formerly known as Middleton Old Hall, a key was discovered under the main doorway during the rebuilding phase. It had been placed there to deter the practitioners of black arts from venturing across the threshold. In the Middle Ages, fear of witchcraft was taken very seriously by the simple-minded folk of the period. A key, together with pots of bent pins, was thought to counter their malignant influence.

   If you intend to finish this walk with a meal at the Old Rooftree Inn, then make use of their car park. I can whole-heartedly recommend such an option with confidence. The key, a large iron implement, is kept on display behind the bar for all to see.

The Walk

Stroll past the side of the inn up Low Lane until it bends to the right. A signpost on the left points the way to Overton down a short passage stiled at either end. Fork half left over to an isolated ladder stile and follow the hedge round as it swings to the right. Mount a stile at the terminus of the field and continue alongside the hedge heading south east across the flat mossland. This section can be a bit muddy after heavy rain.

Straddle another stile at the end of this field then follow a hedge right for 100 metres to the next stile. Stick with the hedge on your right for another 100 metres until you reach one shooting off west in the adjacent field. Stop here and bear left across the open stretch of grassland to a stile on the far side.

After this, bear half right aiming for the left side of the sewage works. Walk down the side by a stout wire fence to emerge onto the service road through a gate. Fork into the farm access road after 50 metres and head left towards the edge of Overton chaperoning the flood control embankment on your right. Emerging opposite The Globe, you should head right onto Lades Marsh. The road continues onward to Sunderland Point subject to tidal constraints.

Our route forks left along the side of Brazil promontory. Mount a substantial ladder stile on the left to make a direct ascent of the easy grass bank onto the hill above, crowned by a trig column. Excellent views are afforded towards Sunderland Point, isolated on the far side of the Lune estuary. Next head south across the grassy sward to mount a hedge stile. Then bear half right through a broken line of trees down a gently shelving grass slope to a hedge stile below.

Beyond this follow the hedge on your left down to another giving

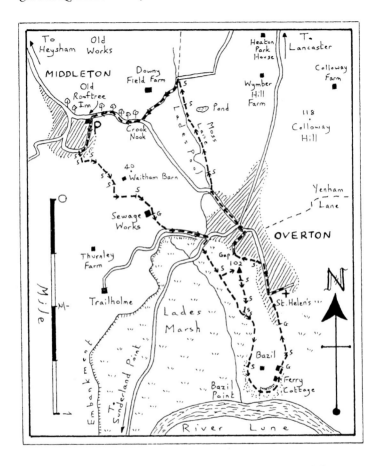

onto the foreshore. Here you need to swing immediately left over a small stile to follow the embankment around in a wide sweep until a stile is reached, depositing you on the shore for the walk around Brazil Point. This is a stony section but even at high tide you should have no problem getting round to the far side. Along this section you can see old fishing huts that are still in regular use.

Just beyond a fence and stile is Ferry Cottage from which passage

Overton church and its original Norman doorway.

across the swirling waters was at one time regularly made to Glasson Dock. By road the length of the journey through Lancaster reaches double figures. At the next cottage, leave the shore by a gate and follow the access track along to the outer suburbs of Overton. Walk up this past a row of new houses.

On reaching the paved road corner, head right for a visit to what is reputed to be Lancashire's oldest church in regular use.

The thick walls of St Helens have withstood the fierce elements since the ninth century. The ancient door positioned within its round Anglo-Norman stone archway has been dated back to the eleventh century. The church is located amidst modern housing. This strange enigma resulted from an ever-changing coastline in the days before flood control measures were introduced. This led to the original village huts being moved to more solid ground where the older part of the village now stands.

Leave the church walking back to the corner and bearing right for 200 metres taking a narrow passage that forks left into the fields behind the houses.

Keep onward when the path becomes paved eventually emerging close to the main village crossroads. Bear left initially, then cross straight over and take the road to Heysham. Immediately beyond the last house, slant right along a track beside Lades Pool.

Mount a stile and accompany an indistinct route in a direct line that chaperones the stream. After passing a pond on the right, straddle a stile soon after joining the Lancaster road. Head left merging with the Heysham road at Crook Nook. A brief stroll to the right will return you to the Old Roof Tree.

Intrigue and mystery emanate from the Old Roof Tree Inn at Middleton.

Eye of the Conder

River and canal play host to a walk where fond memories surge to the fore

Distance: 6 miles

Height: 100 feet (30 metres)

Start/finish: Make use of the car park and picnic site at Conder Green adjoining the River Lune

Terrain: Rolling hedged fields between the Lancaster Canal and Lune estuary

Explorer 296 *Lancaster and Morecambe*

Shops etc.: Glasson Dock

Prelude

Prior to setting off on this local walk, climb to the top of the grass banking beside the river. Before you stretches the broad reach of the widening River Lune as it approaches the estuary. A mile of marsh and mudflats separates us from Overton on the far shore rising only slightly above the level of the flood plain. This locality was visited on our previous walk, number nine. To the left is Glasson Dock where cargo vessels still unload. Upstream lies the city of Lancaster, out of sight around the bend.

A more tranquil scene is difficult to envisage so near to the distraction of urban living. All manner of bird life scoot across the flats dipping effortlessly to secure a tasty morsel for lunch. Fishermen still ply these waters, the river being cleaner now than at any time in living memory. Whitebait, sprats and flounder together with the much-revered salmon find their way into nets strung across the estuary.

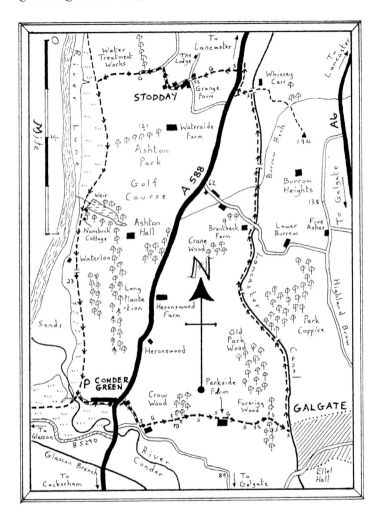

The Walk

Stroll back along the lane swinging left past the old viaduct. Now a footbridge, it once carried the railway branch line from Lancaster to Glasson Dock across the River Conder.

Like all rivers nearing their exit, the Conder swings in a series of constricted meanders before merging with the mighty Lune. Across the marshy reed beds, numerous old boats lie strewn about like beached whales.

Stone cottages line the road above the level of the marshes to avoid flooding at high tide. Most renowned in the locality is the last building. The Stork Hotel has catered for the needs of hungry travellers for over four centuries. The famed diarist Tyldesley referred to it in his writing when he called for a drink in 1712.

Your intrepid guide's own affection for this old pub cannot be understated. It provided a first-class wedding reception in 1971 and a silvery celebration of equal standard twenty-five years later. Both my wife and I will always have the fondest of memories for this fine hostelry.

Take the first right immediately after the Stork and watch for a signpost on the left pointing the way east to Galgate and the canal. Mount the stile passing left of Websters Farm. Enter the next field and make your way over to the right hand edge of Crow Wood. Straddle a stile followed by a small footbridge. Another twenty metres and the next stile finds you continuing on an easterly course.

With a hedge on your left, the indistinct path rises gradually on the approach to a hedge with an old iron ladder stile tucked away on the left. Into the adjoining field, drop down to Parkside Farm where a gap stile allows passage through the yard. Exit via a gate at the far side to accompany a hedge now on your right. At the first gap, change to the far side of the hedge dropping down to a rough triangle of grass.

Keep to the left side of this small enclosure stiled at each side. Then mount the facing grass knoll. Over the far side of the field, drop down to enter Forerigg Wood via a fence stile. A thin trail meanders down between the trees to exit at the bottom by way of another stile. Bearing right, amble down to the edge of the wood to make a diagonal crossing of this field to gain the canal towpath. Now head north towards Lancaster.

> *The village over the far side of the canal is Galgate which came to prominence with its prestigious silk mill. Textile manufacture has long since departed but the mills still remain in a variety of guises. Today, Galgate is best known for its marina where many canal craft are moored.*

At Bridge 50, climb the steps at the side to join the cross track heading left to reach the A588. Take a right for 200 metres keeping an eye open for the Stodday signpost on the far side. A little-used right-of-way, the stile giving access to an adjacent field is often hidden by overgrown nettles in summer.

Ascend the field keeping to the right side of a hedge passing through a gate at the top end. Drop down the far side where a double stile

The Stork.

Craft of all types are moored at Galgate Marina.

hidden from view enables you to gain the village road. This is another one where care may need to be exercised if sensitive regions of the anatomy are to remain untainted. On my last visit thick prickly holly abounded.

Secluded and relatively unknown, Stodday exudes an atmosphere of timeless appeal. Head downhill past a row of pretty cottages swinging sharp right to reach a T-junction. Bear left there past the sewage works now euphemistically termed a water treatment facility. Soon after we pass by a gate, it becomes a track that leads down to the banks of the Lune. Here we join the course of the old railway opened in 1883.

The railway effectively sealed the fate of the Glasson branch of the canal carrying industrial products to and from Lancaster at a much faster rate of knots. The decline of Glasson as a major supply port was hastened by the arrival of the motorway which led to the railway closing down in 1964.

55

Today it is a favourite local footpath and the canal has seen a resurgence of interest as a leisure facility. Such is progress which has now come full circle.

Head south along this fine gravel track back towards Conder Green, the only indication of its past use being a bridge that we pass beneath close to Waterloo Cottage. Half way along this section, we pass a lake on the left which forms part of Lancaster Golf Club.

Ashton Hall, a Jacobean residence which is now the clubhouse, is said to harbour a ghost known as the White Lady. The story is told of certain Lord Ashton who incarcerated his wife in the tower before setting off for the wars.

He was a jealous fellow who zealously intended to preserve his wife's virtue by such a dire action. Due to an unforeseen delay, he returned home later than expected only to find that she had passed away. Thereafter, the unfortunate lady's ghost was seen wandering around the tower on windy moonlit nights.

Bentham's mammoth guardian

Stuck on the edge of bleak moorland, the Great Stone exudes a pagan magnetism that positively crackles

Distance: 8 miles
Height: 650 feet (198 metres)

Start/finish: At Low Bentham, turn off the B6480 past the Punch Bowl Inn and park 50 metres up the lane on the wide verge on the left

Terrain: Rolling grass pastures surrender to the more austere appearance of wild moorlands as height is gained on the rising slopes of the fells.

Explorer OL41 *Forest of Bowland*
(This is the most complicated walk in this book so the OS map is especially recommended)

Shops etc.: High Bentham

Prelude

Extensive grass pastures populated by sheep and cattle occupy the lower slopes that surround the Forest of Bowland. As one nears the 700 foot contour, the pastoral scenery of cultivated farmland, surrounded by fencing and hedgerows, abruptly changes. And there it is, grimly austere, wild and lonely. The bleak wilderness that personifies the Bowland Fells. Few paths venture across this remote tract and roads merely nudge the outer edges.

The two settlements that comprise Low and High Bentham nestle on the lower northern frontier in the valley of the River Wenning. High Bentham has become the main village, more akin to a town with a bustling main street and railway station. At a point where a variety

of roads meet, industries associated with milling grew up along the riverbanks. Today it is tourism that is the main focus of commercial activity with a huge caravan park spreading along both sides of the Wenning to the west of the township.

The focus of this particular walk is a huge entity, the exact location of which I have only recently discovered. The Great Stone of Fourstones is a mighty chunk of grey rock isolated amidst the undulating ocean of moorland sedges. This mystical monolith is a remnant from the Ice Age deposited by the receding ice sheet thousand of years ago in this remote locale.

Indeed there is no other way that such a beast can have come to rest here so far removed from its fellows. Unless of course you accede to the suggestion that it was dropped by Old Nick when he was building the Devil's Bridge at Kirkby Lonsdale.

With an ancient right-of-way aiming directly for this gargantuan grandee, one has to assume that it was regarded with awe and mystery by locals in past epochs. Another claim to nobility is that the stone lies exactly on the boundary betwixt Lancaster and North Yorkshire.

Low Bentham in the Wenning valley.

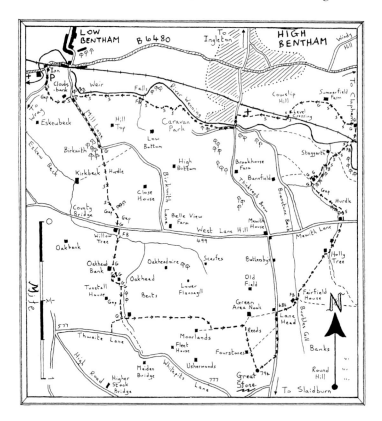

The Walk

Our walk begins with a short stroll up Eskew Lane forking left over a stile into a playing field after only 50 metres. Accompany the hedge on your right in a wide left-hand sweep passing through a hedge gap after 100 metres. Keep below Cloudsbank to join Mill Lane. Take a right up here for a half-mile. Then at a sharp left hander, keep on ahead through a gate aiming for the far right corner of the field where a hidden fence hurdle is mounted.

Keep heading south to the far side of this field negotiating a fence stile. After this veer right to join a wall with another stile at the end. Wander alongside a hedge on your right through a line of trees bearing away left to pass through another gap to reach West Lane Hill.

The path continues offset to the left up the access track serving Oakhead Bank, one of numerous isolated settlements that refer to this mighty English tree. Take the gate on the left some 50 metres this side of the house through a field to circumvent the farmyard. Aim half right over to a gate cutting back right to rejoin the original track beyond.

After passing through the final gate when the track becomes metalled, bear right through another gate to mount the left side of the tree-lined cutting occupied by County Beck. Half way up the incline, pass through a fence gap. A further 150 metres will bring you to a gate opening onto a walled track. Now cross County Beck and up the far side past through a gate adjoining an isolated house.

Make your way due east over a tract of rough moorland known as Bents. After a half-mile when the accompanying wall on your right leans away, follow it round to join a substantial track serving Moorlands. Keep heading east for a quarter mile until you reach a wall corner. Bear hard right sticking close to the wall through a rough cluster of reeds.

On reaching the Fourstones access track, continue ahead over open rough ground to merge with the Great Stone 200 metres ahead. Unmissable amidst the rolling waves of grass, the monument is soon reached close to a fence marking the Lancashire/North Yorkshire county boundary.

> *Pitted with the etched names of past visitors, a flight of steps up to the apex have been carved into the giant boulder. Especially to the north the view is amazing with the 'Three Peaks' of Ingleborough, Whernside and Pen-y-Ghent vying for attention. To the east, the windswept moors of Bowland disappear over the gently swelling horizon.*

From here, take the path heading north east angling down to join

Awesome and mind-boggling! – The Great Stone of Fourstones.

the open fell road. Stroll down to Lane Head swinging right along a track to Fairfield House. Cross the deep cutting of Burbles Gill by a footbridge heading downstream for 50 metres before forking left over the rough grass. Take a bend on Holly Tree further down merging with the paved access road and wandering down this to Mewith Lane.

Continue down an overgrown path to the right side of the house opposite. Mount a stile after 100 metres bearing left to head in a north westerly direction. After mounting a fence hurdle across the path, accompany the tree-lined gill down to the farming settlement of Branstone Beck. Go through a gap and drop down to cross the beck via two gates. The continuing path lies on the far side of the house. Bear right through a gate and a back garden to rejoin Branstone Beck.

Stroll down this left bank. Lower down, cross to the far side by a footbridge followed soon after by a fence stile. Pick your way down this side of the gill over another footbridge and stile to emerge into a

61

large open field. Head down towards the River Wenning in the valley bottom crossing a major field track. Following more stiles in quick succession, you will be able to straddle the river by a substantial footbridge.

Pass under the railway to mount the facing slope to Ridding Lane Farm. Above the farm, bear left through a gate wandering along the bottom edge of a field now heading due west. After mounting a stile, aim half right towards a stile in the hedge ahead. Keep going steadily uphill over two more stiles to reach Summerfield Farm. Stay below the buildings passing through a gate after which the path swings downhill to re-cross the railway.

Head west on the far side to reach St Margaret's Church in High Bentham. Bear left along a road taking the first right on the far side of the Wenning at Bentham Bridge. Joining the river trail after 200 metres, the path passes through the Riverside Caravan Park. Watch for a sharp left away from the river where the path is directed above the development.

Mount a couple of fence stiles close together then accompany the fence on your right down to the riverside. A notched gully is straddled by a stile and footbridge. Keep following the river downstream with a wall stile after 300 metres. Another footbridge then a stile after 100 metres will find you approaching Mill Lane through a thin screen of trees. Go straight over the road to accompany the outward path back to Low Bentham.

At Holme with the dolphins

An unusually beautiful setting in the Wyre Valley enabled the textile industry to flourish

Distance: 6 miles
Height: 250 feet (76 metres)

Start/finish: The car park adjoining the village hall in Upper Dolphinholme

Terrain: Rolling grass pastures split by the deep valley of the River Wyre

Explorer OL41 *Forest of Bowland*

Shops etc.: Upper Dolphinholme

Prelude

There can only be a handful of settlements in the North West that are divided into three distinct parts. Dolphinholme is one of these, with two upper sections and a lower one in the valley bottom of the River Wyre. Originally named from a single farm on the south side of the valley, it grew up where the River Wyre bubbled and chattered its way through a gorge below the site of the present village.

Here it was that a mill was built complete with adjacent cottages for the workers. The deep cutting riven out by the Wyre as it flows off the Bowland Fells was ideal for powering one of the new breed of mills that spurred the Industrial Revolution.

A huge waterwheel turned the machinery that produced cotton and worsted cloth before the advent of steam power made it redundant. It was one of the tallest water wheels in Britain. At 68 feet in diameter and 12 feet broad, the wheel was second only to the fine specimen that still operates, if only for tourists, at Laxey in the Isle of Man. After the mill finally closed its doors in 1867, the wheel was blown up and no remains can be found.

Hundreds of workers were employed in the mill and extra cottages were needed to house them. At its height, the village had over 3,000 residents, with almost half working in the mill. These were built in the village proper and can be seen in the older section of Upper Dolphinholme. Such was its importance as an industrial settlement that Dolphinholme became one of the first places in the county to have its very own gas supply.

The Walk

But first we must set out from the newer section of the village by walking down the road past the old mill cottages and turning right 50 metres beyond the first junction. Accompany the paved pathway left down to the lower part of the village. The mill has now been converted into several residences. After crossing the stone bridge in the old heart of the lower village, the Wagon Road swings uphill bending left beside a wood on the left.

Mill cottages in Upper Dolphinholme.

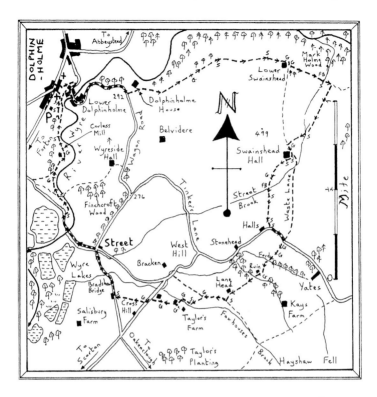

Emerging onto the upper pastures, watch for the access road serving Dolphinholme House Farm on the left. Follow a clear track up a rising gradient until a gate is reached. Beyond this, continue ahead above the valley floor alongside an intermittent line of trees. Straddling a fence stile, circle right to another beyond which is a barn.

Still heading due east along another line of thorn trees mount a stile at the end. Then aim half left passing through a fence gap to reach Lower Swainshead. Go through a gate into the farmyard and another on the left beside a clutch of conifers.

Follow a grass path aiming to end up 200 metres above the limit of Mark Holme Wood when it fades. Cross the fence keeping ahead for

50 metres before crossing a fence by means of a footbridge and stile. Keep ahead bearing hard right after 50 metres to join a fence a little further along and accompany it to a stile. Over this make a half left to mount a shallow gradient to reach Swainshead Hall.

Avoid the paved access road known as Waste Lane by bearing right down a grass track to locate the stile on the right allowing you to cross a walled lawn. Make your way over the open field dropping down to a gate followed by a footbridge crossing Street Brook. Go up the facing slope to mount a stile and follow a fence all the way to a back lane gained by surmounting two more stiles.

Head left for 200 metres then take a right through a gate where Waste Lane continues as a sunken grassy corridor. This must have been a major farm connecting track in days gone by, now abandoned just like the farms. Beyond the next gate, straddle a ford leaning left on the far side. Another 100 metres will find you at a gate followed by a ruined farmhouse on the right.

Pick your way over another ford continuing onward past yet another abandoned farm to reach a footpath T-junction. Head right for 200 metres forking left along a fence when a gate is reached. This will bring you to Foxhouses Brook. Mount a stile on the right followed by a gate downstream to cross over the brook. Climb out of the tree-lined cutting to join the track serving Taylor's Farm.

Walk down this slanting left along Long Lane. After only 50 metres, go through a gate on the right heading due west across an open field. Make toward the mid-point of the houses in front to join another lane. Bear right down to a crossroads given the name of Street. Take a left here past a series of commercial fishing lakes.

After crossing Street Bridge, watch for a stile in the hedge on your right. Cross the field to join the wooded bank of the River Wyre. Accompany the river upstream past the bridge giving access to the rear of Wyreside Hall, seen overlooking the valley on the far side. Continue along the river bank for 200 metres passing through a gate at the edge of some woods.

The path soon merges with the track serving Corless Mill now converted to residences. Keep to the right of these through a gate,

The old mill beside the River Wyre.

strolling over a level grass pasture to the far side of a field where a stile allows entry to some woods.

Leave this lower path after 300 metres forking left up a delightful path through the tree cover emerging above by a fence stile. Make a diagonal ascent of the grass slope to reach Upper Dolphinholme close to the parish church of St Mark. Head left through the churchyard and so back to the main street.

In the company of monks and shepherds

Emotive contrasts of beauty and tragedy in a single breath

Distance: 4.5 miles

Height: 300 feet (92 metres)

Start/finish: Park on the grass verge opposite the entrance to the Shepherds' Church located one mile before Abbeystead

Terrain: Rolling foothills stretching down from the Bowland Fells with indistinct paths on grass

Explorer OL41 *Forest of Bowland*

Shops etc.: Dolphinholme

Prelude

An unspoilt rural utopia is an apt description for the area around the Wyre Valley near Abbeystead. Footpaths are little used in this remote corner of Lancashire, which is far removed from the usual tourist trails. Here ramblers can leave their problems in the car to enjoy a splendid walk of rustic charm amidst undeniable solitude.

Feeder streams draining off the Bowland Fells converge at Abbeystead which is often referred to as Emmetts, an influential title adopted by woods, houses and even an isolated Methodist church. No secret is the origin of the settlement dating from the twelfth century when Cistercian monks established an abbey in the valley. Finding this to be a bleak and inhospitable site during the long winters, they soon decamped and headed for Ireland. The name is all that remains to indicate the existence of this religious association.

Today the tiny village comprises naught but a cluster of houses and a school dating back to 1674 when 'Cawthorne's Endowed School' was set up. The first teacher was selected because of his religious zeal and *for being 'no tippler nor haunter of alehouses'. Many of the buildings however date from the Victorian era when they were built by the Earl of Sefton, who was the major landowner hereabouts.*

The Walk

To commence our walk, cross the road and stroll down the drive to the church. When passing the over Wyresdale war memorial, take special note of the adjoining seat dedicated to Felix Dugdale. A long lost relative of your exalted guide perhaps? Go through the lychgate with its poignant claim that 'I am the door of the sheep'.

> *This is the Shepherds' Church where generations of woolly wardens have hung their crooks in the porch before the morning service. Stained glass windows illustrate the importance attached to our curly-coated colleagues in the local economy.*

Pass through a gate at the back of the churchyard to drop down a field aiming half right to a footbridge giving access to the adjoining field by means of a double fence stile. Mount a short banking at the top of which is sited an unusual arrowed marker post carved in stone.

From here head due west across an open field towards Lentworth Hall. Veer towards a wall on the right and accompany it over to a fence stile. Make a left turn from here through the farmyard passing through a stile and gate at the end. Beyond this, keep the fence on your right down to another gate. Thereafter it is on your left as you arrive at a fenced wood.

Follow the wood down to cross a major field track stiled at either side. Descend the short continuation of Long Wood by means of some stone steps bearing left to head upstream along the lower terraces of the River Wyre.

With a fence on your right, and a low banking to the left, stroll along this grassy sward to reach a small copse after a half mile. At the far side is a gate and footbridge where we merge with the field track continuing on to reach the pumping station.

> *It is difficult to imagine how tranquillity and tragedy can be so closely interwoven in this remote location. Yet on 23 May*

This church is dedicated to shepherds.

1984, a methane gas build-up caused an explosion in the subterranean galleries of catastrophic proportions. Pause in silent tribute to the 16 visitors from St Michaels-on-the-Wyre who died here on that horrendous day.

Then continue on towards the iron footbridge keeping this side of the River Wyre and climbing up through the trees to join the top of the dam. Victorian engineers recognised the importance of the Wyre Valley as a source of water for the growing towns of North Lancashire back in 1853 when the dam was built. So well has it blended with the surrounding landscape that only the stone ramparts of the containing walls reveal it as a man-made facility.

Return to the bridge, crossing over to accompany the opposite side

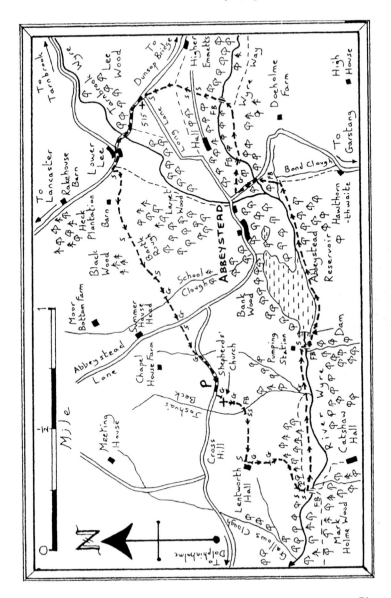

A stone-carved direction marker points the way.

of the river along a clear path. Climb above the magnificent fanned overflow and onward through the woods beside the reed-choked reservoir. As part of the *Wyre Way*, the lakeside path eventually reaches a footbridge in Hinberry Wood close to the confluence of both Tarnbrook and Marshaw Wyre rivers. Another 100 metres will find you merging into a back lane.

Bear left for 100 metres to fork right along a sign-posted path. To visit the village of Abbeystead, carry on to the T-junction and bear left. Our way passes through a gate keeping to the right side of a large field. Just beyond a wooden shelter at its far end, cross a footbridge over the Marshaw Wyre to slant left up a rising bank. Keep midway between the river and intermittent clusters of trees on the slopes above.

> To your left is the imposing structure of Abbeystead Hall maintaining a watchful eye on the valley as it has done since 1887. The Earl of Sefton did much to revitalise the Wyre Valley entertaining royalty in his new mansion and providing grouse shoots on the surrounding moors. Many of the finest meets were held during the reign of George V who was himself a first-class shot.

> One story tells of a young beater called George Drinkall who one day inadvertently found himself in the shooting line. On hearing the warning cry of 'Look out, George!' from all sides, it was the King himself who ducked. The height of game shooting at Abbeystead Hall was in 1915 when almost 3,000 birds were shot. One shudders to think what the cry would be today if such a situation were re-enacted.

After passing the Hall, drop down to re-cross the river by another footbridge. On the far side climb out of the enclosing trees alongside a wall on your left. The thin path soon zigzags up a steep banking though the loose tree cover onto flatter ground above. Bear away right from the wooded surroundings across a short field to reach the fenced access road serving the Hall.

Cross straight over into the adjoining field by two ladder stiles and follow a fence on the right along to join the main road that traverses the Trough of Bowland. We join this road at its junction with Long Lane which heads left down towards Abbeystead.

Head left past Emmetts Church down the road into the valley of Tarnbrook Wyre. After a half mile and after passing through the hamlet of Lower Lee, barely more than a handful of cottages, watch for the start of two sign-posted footpaths just beyond a bend in the road.

Take the far one over a wall stile circling left through a line of trees before mounting a gradual grass slope in a westerly direction out of the valley. Keep 100 metres to the left of a prominent barn joining a beck from the left and accompanying this to its source. You should soon arrive at a fence. Straddle the stile then follow another fence on your left until it can be crossed by the first stile reached.

Continue on the opposite side of this fence to join a field track. This crosses a stream known as School Clough before passing through a gate and continuing in a straight line to cross straight over Abbeystead Lane. A stile enables you to cross the next field to its far-left corner where a small gate brings you onto the main valley road. A quarter mile walk to the right will then return you to the Shepherds' Church.

Good tidings from Pilling

Find out how smugglers contributed to the development of tide tables at Pilling

Distance: 6.5 miles
Height: Insignificant

Start/finish: Bear right at Pilling and drive for 1.5 miles to the end of Fluke Hall Lane where a car park is located on the edge of the sands

Terrain: Flat drained mossland with many fields separated by fences

Explorer 296 *Lancaster, Morecambe and Fleetwood*

Shops etc.: Pilling

Prelude

Tucked away on the north coast of the Fylde, Pilling can only be accessed via numerous roads that twist and turn across the mossland. The name is of Celtic origin meaning 'a small creek' ,which implies that there was once a harbour here. That has long since been absorbed by the mossland. Pilling's attraction is for people who enjoy the quiet life. At one time the mosslands were subject to frequent floods. But in 1830, extensive drainage work was undertaken which has left the area with rich soils. Pilling potatoes are a prized export to all parts of the North West. Although a tranquil backwater today, smugglers and wreckers once lured unwary ships to their doom on the treacherous sands.

Only when a local priest called George Holden devised a set of tide tables was the evil trade stopped. A mathematical genius, the Reverend Holden was vicar at Pilling for nine years from 1758. He remains one of Lancashire's unsung heroes.

Unreliability of the narrow moss roads for movement of farm produce to market was substantially improved with the railway extension

The windmill with no sails is now a prestigious residence.

from Garstang. Known as The Pilling Pig, the steam engine traversed a line that has long since been dismantled but can easily be picked out on the map. An example of these old locomotives has recently been sited at Fold House Caravan Park.

Another unusual feature can be seen if you are travelling to Pilling from the direction of Lancaster. Just before crossing Broadfleet Bridge on the left is an old windmill minus cap and sails. Dating from 1808, it was converted to steam-power in the 1880s and finally stopped grinding corn in 1926. Today it makes an attractive private residence.

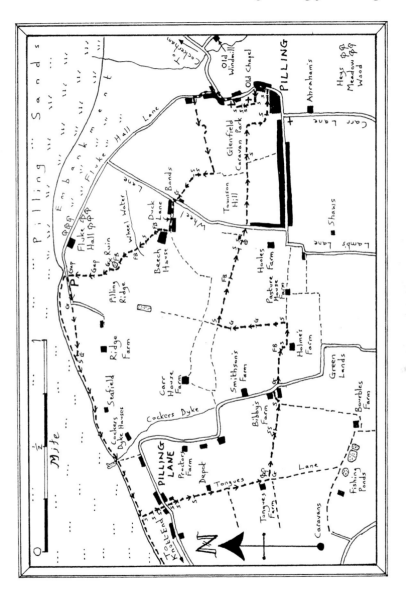

The Walk

Begin this ramble from the car park by continuing along the coast road until it swings sharply inland. This is the access road to Ridge Farm. Continue ahead through gate into a field accompanying the hedge as it veers towards the embankment. Join this paved walkway heading west. The view across the sands towards the Lake District is far reaching.

After passing the outflow of Cocker's Dyke into the Bay, watch for a signed path below the embankment. Mount four stiles walking along the left side of a field to reach Pilling Lane. The road and the scattered settlement have the same name.

Go straight across through a stile beside a reedy dyke. Keep heading south down a narrow fenced passage into a field with a stile at its far end.

Go past a transport depot to join a paved road serving Tongues House on the right. When the road becomes rough, negotiate a gate on the left and walk alongside a fenced dyke to reach Bibby's Farm. A double stile has to be straddled midway along.

Bear left over a stile to walk through the farmyard into a lane. Bear right then left after 50 metres through a gate. Keep heading east to reach Holme's farm. After a footbridge and hidden stile on the left, keep to the right side of the next field. At its far side mount a stile veering north passing through two gates.

About 100 metres beyond the second, watch for a stile in the hedge enabling you to continue heading east. A direct course over a footbridge and two stiles will bring you to Wheel Lane. Cross straight over, soon entering the back of Glenfield Caravan Park. Follow the service road to its entrance. Opposite a derelict farm, go through a stile on the left to stroll behind housing to reach Pilling's main street.

Bear left for 200 metres along the road then left again to visit the old eighteenth century chapel and its well tended graveyard.

> *Now owned by English Heritage, it is still used by parishioners on selected dates during the year. Should you wish to peruse*

the inner sanctum, an address is given where the key can be obtained.

This is the chapel where George Holden preached and the striking sundial above the doorway is dedicated to his memory. A paved walkway behind connects with the newer inspired church.

No excuse for being late to chapel in Pilling.

Rejoin the main street continue along this for 200 metres before slanting left into Fluke Hall Lane. Head left at the first sign-posted path. Entering a field, follow the hedge round to the left until a wide gap allows you to enter the next field. Slant right here straddling two stiles which will bring you onto a large grass pasture. bear half left aiming for a white building at the far side. A gate and ladder stile allow passage through the property to rejoin Wheel Lane.

Bear right for 50 metres then left into Dock Lane. At the end of the lane, enter the grounds of Beech House on the right where a narrow passage at the rear will bring you into the field behind by means of a footbridge. Cross to the far left corner and another stile. Keep bearing to the left over two footbridges to reach the abandoned settlement of Pilling Ridge. This is now just a huddle of ruins.

Go round the left edge of a pond passing through a gate. Keep to the left side of the next field heading due north. Two gaps in field hedges will then return you to the car park this side of the coastal embankment.

Murder on the Wyre

Even the most tranquil of locales conceals its own macabre secrets

Distance: 6.5 miles
Height: Insignificant

Start/finish: Entering Hambleton from the north along the main A588, pull off left down Sandy Lane when the road takes a sharp right. Park on the left close to the United Reform Church

Terrain: Flat land of the Wyre used for mixed farming and scored by numerous rights-of-way that are frequently indistinct and overgrown due to lack of use

Explorer 296 *Lancaster, Morecambe and Fleetwood*

Shops etc.: Hambleton

Prelude

For 300 years up to the early eighteenth century, Hambleton was noted for its thriving salt industry. The tides played a vital part in this process, allowing the brine to settle in hollows which were raked after drying out. Saltwelling was the boiling process undertaken in long low sheds as a secondary occupation by local farmers.

The industry declined rapidly with the mining of cheap salt found beneath the Cheshire plain. Today the village is a commuter settlement for people working in Blackpool. Farming is still an important occupation, with cattle and sheep prospering on the rich grassland. Pig farming used to be a major feature of the Wyre, but only one working farm now remains due to the import of cheap pork from abroad.

One gruesome tale that has long fascinated local people is that concerning a certain Richard Pedder. One day in April of 1853 he charged into the Shovels Inn on the main street and announced that he had done away with his wife with a shotgun. Returning to his house followed by a crowd of locals, he threw himself down beside the blood-

stained corpse. Weeping and bemoaning his loss, he then tried to take his own life but was prevented. A policeman then conveyed Pedder to the lock-up at Stamine. No reason was ever given for this uncharacteristic act and many thought it was an accident while Pedder's mind was disturbed – a moment of rashness that resulted in such dire consequences. But this plea by the defence failed to convince the jury at his trial in Lancaster and a verdict of 'wilful murder' was passed. Even though the jury added a recommendation for mercy, the judge had no hesitation in passing the ultimate sentence. Even a petition containing some 530 signatures failed to move the authorities.

Sentence of death by hanging was duly carried out at noon on 27 August in the year 1853 outside Lancaster Castle. As no execution had been witnessed for eighteen years, the macabre event attracted many voyeurs from the surrounding districts. Well before the designated hour, Castle Parade was teeming. Many of the local factories shut down, more to deliver a moral lesson to their employees than as concession to their morbid curiosity. The silent crowd slowly dispersed after the hanging when the body was cut down and interred within the precincts of the prison.

The Shovells at Hambleton where a murderer confessed.

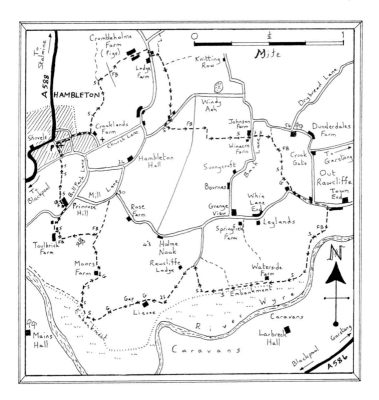

The Walk

Cast these unwholesome thoughts from your mind as you set off up the back lane to the left of the United Reform Church. At the top, bear left then right. After 20 metres, slant left along a hedged track. When the field opens out, chaperone a fence bending left but watch for a stile that allows you to cross the field aiming for Crombleholme Farm. This is the last pig farm left on the Wyre. A sad reflection on the state of British farming when most of our pork has to be imported.

Pass through the farmyard heading right down Sower Carr Lane and take a rough track on the left after 100 metres. Accompany this round

83

The United Reformed church at Hambleton.

to the right all the way along to the next lane. Head right here for another 100 metres, there mounting a stile on the left.

Pass beneath overhead power lines heading due east across a field to cross a dyke via a footbridge. Continue heading east but cross right to accompany a hedge along to a stile at the start of a narrow hedged passage. Arriving at Back Lane, cross straight over to another stile in the hedge.

Following another soon after you will reach a wide hedged corridor. Follow this all the way down to another lane. Angle left for a quarter mile until a signpost on the right at Town End points the way south to the River Wyre. At the end of a hedged and overgrown corridor, a stile gives access to the riverside.

Head right downstream over a footbridge. After straddling the first stile stick closely to the hedge/fence following it all the way to Waterside Farm. At this point continue in a westerly direction on the embankment up to the second stile.

Join a hedged track heading inland up to a T-junction. Bear left to reach the isolated farmsteads of Liscoe. Keep right of a barn to pass through a gate. Head due west with the hedge on your left across three fields. A stile hidden on the far side of the last field gives access to river embankment.

Cross a stile almost immediately, strolling onward for another 100 metres until the next one is reached. Mount this to head inland alongside a hedge up to the stile at the far side of the field. Now aim half right to a gate giving access to Moors Farm. Go through the yard and down the access road for a quarter mile.

Watch for a stile pointing the way left to Toulbrick Farm. As you get nearer, a stile in the hedge on your right allows passage over the adjacent field to gain the access road. Stroll along this to reach Bull Park Lane. Bear right for 100 metres then take a left alongside Primrose Hill.

After passing a pond, and opposite the pheasant farm, mount the stile in the hedge on your right aiming half left. Maintain a straight course mounting two more field edge stiles to reach back Church Lane on the edge of Hambleton. Take a right for 50 metres then left along Sandy Lane back to the start.

Scorton's guardian angel

Industry and religion compete with scenic splendour in the foothill shadows

Distance: 5 miles
Summit: Nicky Nook, 705 feet
Height: 650 feet (198 metres)

Start/finish: Ample roadside parking to the south of Scorton village adjacent to the public toilets

Terrain: Deep cut valleys and rough moorland rise up behind Scorton to merge with the Bowland Fells

Explorer OL41 *Forest of Bowland*

Shops etc.: Scorton

Prelude

Behind Scorton, the hill country begins quite abruptly, in marked contrast to the flatness characteristic of the Fylde. Lying off the main north–south route, Scorton has become something of a honey pot, attracting all manner of visitors including cyclists, day-trippers, and, of course, walkers.

Clichés such as picturesque, sleepy, unspoilt, and enchanting slip off the tongue when folk refer to Scorton's charm. The village possesses all those essential elements that unite to make up the ideal English village. But one thing it lacks is a traditional local pub.

There is, however, a gift shop and restaurant called The Priory that serves alcoholic beverages. As such it attracts a large clientele during any fine weekend when sightseers call in for a snack. Although The Priory might not have any religious connection these days, it was at one time the home of the local Catholic priest. Even today, the vil-

lage most certainly enjoys a strong ecclesiastical presence with three churches represented.

The most obvious is St Peter's founded in 1879 with its prominent spire soaring high above the village. For many travellers motoring along the M6, this slate-clad pinnacle is a landmark informing them that Lancaster is not far distant. And just around the next bend is another striking motorway edifice where refreshment can be obtained at Lancaster South (Forton) motorway services.

The Roman Catholic Church of St Mary and St James consecrated in 1861 is not so extrovert. It is to be found up the steep incline of Snow Hill Lane secreted behind the village among some trees. Easiest of access is the Wesleyan Methodist Chapel on the main street. This is oldest of all, dating back to 1842.

Scorton acquired its name from the deep cutting chiselled out by Tithe Barn Brook and other similar features in the vicinity. Although of Anglo-Saxon origin, Scorton was not mentioned in the Domesday Book of the eleventh century commissioned by William the Conqueror. Its first reference dates from 1587 although most development occurred in the late eighteenth and nineteenth centuries. The landowner at that time was the Duke of Hamilton, and it was he who granted land for the building of a school as well as the Wesleyan Chapel.

In 1853 the Duke sold much of the land hereabouts to the Ormerod Family, who had moved here from Bolton. It was they who created the landscaped parkland surrounding Wyresdale Hall and were responsible for St Peter's Church. With a background in textiles, the Ormerods took over a cotton mill at the north end of the village which provided much needed employment for many local people. Closed in 1920, this now derelict structure was also used as a joinery workshop, dairy and clog factory.

The Walk

Stroll down Gubberford Lane towards Garstang for a half-mile making use of the new Millennium footway beside the River Wyre. Rejoin the road close to a sign-posted stile on the far side pointing towards the motorway. Keep to the fence on your left up to Broad Fall. After passing through a fence gate, followed soon after by a stile,

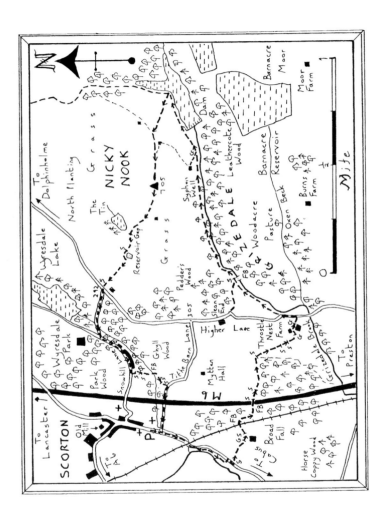

The old cotton mill in Scorton.

strike up a shallow grass rise to reach the railway footbridge. Mount the stile and cross over the line.

On the far side after passing through a gate, bear right along a fenced passage to reach the foot bridge spanning the M6. Beyond a footbridge and double stile, aim half right over to a fence stile at the edge of Woodacre Great Wood. Follow this up to its top end. Mount the second stile on your right slanting away from the woods alongside a reedy dyke. Maintain a straight course over two stiles close together before dropping down to enter Throstle Nest farmyard by a gate. Stroll down to join Higher Lane.

Bear left along here forking right after 50 metres along a clear track, passing through a gate after another 50 metres into the deeply wooded cutting of Grizedale. This enclosed valley forms part of the Bowland Forest Area of Outstanding Natural Beauty, being rich in all

Nicky Nook offers excellent views over the Fylde.

manner of wildlife. Stick with this as it climbs gradually towards the open fell.

About 300 metres beyond the impressive reservoir dam down in the ravine, watch for a clear path bending sharp left to accompany a wall up onto the open fell of Nicky Nook. Keep right of a square stone block to reach the trig column and a spectacular panorama that opens out before you across the Fylde.

The obvious focal point is Blackpool Tower in the far distance. It is little wonder that this is a popular spot on a sunny day.

The grass path continues down the far side of this grassy knoll bearing right past a reservoir with the odd appendage of The Tin on the right.

Go through a wall gap just beyond a group of trees veering left to accompany the wall now on your right past a small reservoir. Beyond a fence stile adjoining the reservoir, the path drops steeply through stands of gorse down to a road junction.

Head downhill taking the right fork along Snowhill Lane, with trees initially on the left, then both sides after crossing Tithe Barn Brook. At the junction, bear left for a quarter mile until a wide dirt track on the left is reached. Down this is a stile giving onto a back field.

Bear right slanting down to another stile giving access to the wooded enclave of Tithe Brook. Drop down to cross a footbridge continuing on the far side. Leave the woods by a stile crossing a short grassy sward to reach Tithe Barn Lane. Then bear right under the motorway passing St Peter's Church on the right on the downward stroll back to Gubberford Lane. Another right will return you to the start.

Mill village
extra-ordinary

Step back into rural Lancashire's industrial past where textile manufacture is still King

Distance: 5.5 miles
Height: 525 feet (160 metres)

Start/finish: Park on the main street of Calder Vale adjacent to the Mission Hall. The mill car park is private and for employees only

Terrain: Rolling foothills and grazing land sliced by the deep cutting of the Calder Valley. Footpaths are indistinct for much of the walk

Explorer OL41 *Forest of Bowland*

Shops etc.: Calder Vale Post Office

Prelude

Emerging from the bleak expanse of the Bowland Fells, the River Calder has carved a bold course through the foothill country of the eastern Fylde to merge with the Wyre at Catterall. The valley explored on this walk is the least known of three Calder Valleys in the north of England, and is in my humble opinion easily the most charming.

It was inevitable that the steeply shelving valley would result in this rural backwater eventually succumbing to industrial exploitation. And so it was that the Jackson Family established their first mill at Calder Vale in 1835 for the purpose of spinning cotton. Although ideal for waterpower, the isolated site meant that a self-contained community was needed. In those early days it was described as 'an oasis amid the hills'.

Rows of terraced houses were erected for the workers. One can

Bottom of the main street in Calder Vale.

only speculate as to why one of them was known as 'Nosey Row'.
They were augmented by a Methodist chapel whose non-conformist
traditions forbade strong drink, the mill owners being Quakers. As a
consequence, the village has never had a pub, though it did have a
Temperance Hotel in addition to three shops and a chippie. Only the
post office/general store remains.

In 1848, Low Mill was built downstream to weave the cotton, the
waste being transported for processing in Oakenclough paper mill.
Both of these have since ceased to operate.

Now owned by an Arabic consortium, the Calder Vale mill still
employs many local people making cotton head-dresses for export to
the mother country. The village's unique location at the road end has
encouraged a special character and atmosphere all its own. You liter-
ally drop into the village down a steep narrow road that terminates
opposite the old manager's house.

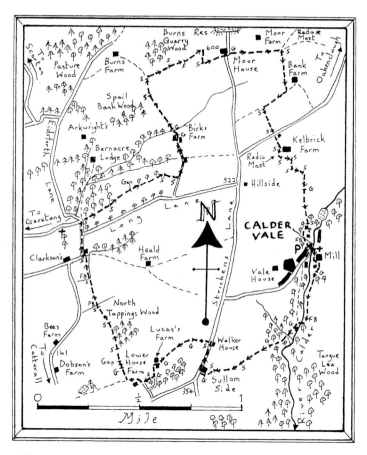

The Walk

Our walk begins by strolling past the mill to head downstream, passing behind a lone cottage and through a gate thereafter joining the river. This section always appears to be somewhat heavy on mud. Keep to the riverside until a substantial footbridge is reached. Cross to the far side and up some steps aiming left past more riverside residences. After 100 metres where the track swings to the left, keep

The mill still operates in Calder Vale.

climbing onward up a narrow trail through the woods away from the river.

Emerge through a gate above to amble alongside a fence on your left to a stile at the end. A fenced corridor then leads down to Strickens Lane with the farm of Sullom Side on the corner. Head right for three hundred metres. Just beyond Walker House, mount the stile on the left accompanying a fence to the end of the field. Pass through a gap veering half left down a gentle slope to locate a gate 50 metres this side of Spring Wood. A short track will find you on the access track serving Lucas's Farm.

Make a left to the edge of Springs Wood then pass through a gate in the hedge on the right. Stroll down to mount a stile after which keep right of Lower House Farm. At the far side near to a stile on the left, bear right across an open field passing through a gate followed soon after by a gap. Keep with the fence on your right over five stiles and two footbridges to reach the access road for Heald Farm.

A left then right for a quarter mile along a lane will bring you to the edge of Helbeck Wood. Do not continue ahead as this is the private estate of Barnacre Lodge. Instead, straddle a double stile to follow the edge of the wood up a gentle slope. Keep onward through a fence gap and bear left over to a line of trees. Accompany this up to a stile. Cross a short section of field and over a fence stile to join the access track for Birks Farm.

Head left to reach the farm, keeping right to avoid the farmhouse. Go through the farmyard in and out of a gate at the back. Drop down to another gate below left before mounting a rising field. Aim for a fence gate 100 metres this side of Spoil Bank Wood. Mount the stile then accompany the next fence on the left to a stile at the field end.

Bear right along a deeply gouged track and over a stile into a field at the end. Drop down to another stile in a depression then climb out up a broad fenced alley swinging sharp right at the top. Beyond a stile, the track heaves left to reach Moor House.

Pass the access road serving Barnacre Reservoir, mounting a step stile in the wall beside a gate. Continue heading east along a rough paved road until a stile on the right allows access to a grass track. This brings us to the edge of Bank Farm. Bend right here down another fenced track until a stile on the left points the way over to Strickens Lane beside the fence on your left.

Cross straight over to stroll up the road serving Kelbrick Farm. A deviation to the right-of-way takes us right to circle around the buildings past a radio mast where a stile is mounted. Over on the far side of the field locate another stile in the hedge, wheeling immediately right to another that finds us on a clear track down to the edge of the next field. Bear right over a stile to follow the hedge, also on your right, heading downhill. At the end of the field go through a gate and keep heading south but with the field fence on your right.

At the upper edge of the wooded Calder Valley, mount a stile bearing right down through the trees past a secluded house on the left. After crossing a footbridge in the woods, drop down to pass between modern houses on the edge of Calder Vale, emerging close to the post office on the main street and a further opportunity to explore this fascinating enclave.

It's great to be little at Eccleston

Being at the centre of things guarantees a place in history

Distance: 6.5 miles
Height: Insignificant

Start/finish: Park in the Square at Great Eccleston.
Avoid Wednesday which is market day and very busy.
An alternative lies close to where the old road rejoins
the by-pass west of the village.

Terrain: Level fields separated by hedges and scattered
clusters of trees epitomises the Fylde landscape

Explorer 296 *Lancaster and Morecambe, 286 Preston and
Blackburn*

Shops etc.: Great Eccleston

Prelude

*Occupying a central position in the Fylde, Great Eccleston has always
played a prominent role in the fortunes of the region. It was even
mentioned in the Domesday Book of William the Conqueror and
named Eglestun, meaning church settlement. Further proof of its
importance was the holding of not one but three annual horse fairs.
The Agricultural Show held in July was founded in 1853 and is one of
the oldest in Lancashire.*

*The Square is where it all happens, including the weekly market.
Old houses mingle with new to create a busy atmosphere, incorporating a wide variety of shops catering for the surrounding community.
Pubs are well represented in Great Eccleston, including both the Black
and White Bulls, which led to it being called 'Little London'. It is also no
doubt a reminder of less genteel sports pursued in yesteryear.*

Leckonby Street heads south from the Square and is named after Richard Leckonby, who in 1783 exhausted his inheritance in a profligate manner. He ended his days in Lancaster Castle, imprisoned for debt. An array of interesting cottages lines the narrow streets on either side of the old core. New developments to the east do not intrude too obviously into the ancient heart of this most attractive of Fylde villages. A stroll round is therefore highly recommended.

The Walk

From the Square, amble west for 200 metres along what was the main road before the by-pass was built. Take a sign-posted path heading left. This soon narrows into a hedged track at the end of which a stile is mounted. Keeping the hedge on your left, straddle three more field

The White Bull — one of numerous hostelries in Great Eccleston.

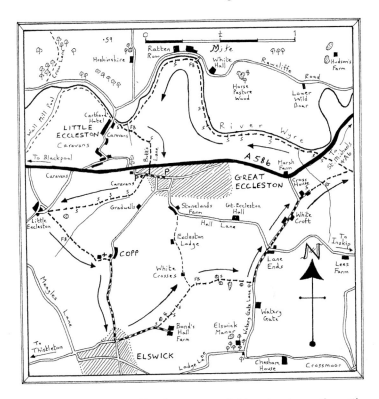

stiles before bearing half right across a field to locate another stile midway along the facing hedge.

Mount this and maintain a straight course to reach the cluster of buildings known as Little Eccleston (not the village). Turn hard left heading south east to cross a slight depression with a footbridge halfway between here and Copp. Keep to the hedge on your left to reach this tiny hamlet. Copp is of Saxon origin stemming from *kopff*, signifying that it occupies a small hill.

The square church tower is a good landmark to guide this part of the walk. St Anne's is passed after bearing left through a gate to amble along a farm access track adjoining the church.

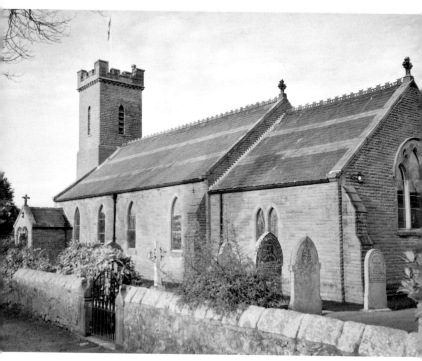

St Ann's at Copp dates back to Saxon times.

Its isolated position chosen in 1723 lies at the mid point between two parishes. The original chapel had a floor of puddled clay and was whitewashed annually from money raised by a levy on pew owners.

Join Copp Lane beside the primary school heading right to reach the outskirts of Elswick.

A village of substantial residential proportions, it lacks the appeal and obvious popularity of Great Eccleston. Being centrally placed makes it an ideal spot from which commuters can travel to work in Blackpool, Preston and beyond. New estates complement the earliest form of planned development along the main street. Small farms provided the principal means of livelihood and later offered accommodation to handloom weavers.

A non-conformist tradition has always been strong throughout The Fylde, and Elswick became a primary focus for dissident religious meetings. But this isolated situation failed to save the odd preacher from a session in the stocks. One of the oldest chapels in the area complete with its seventeenth century foundation stone lies adjacent to the inspired memorial church.

Remoteness from major townships was the reason for Elswick being chosen as the site for a smallpox sanatorium in 1902. Once this disease had been finally eradicated, TB sufferers were sent there until radical improvements in public health provision saw Hoole House changed into a probation hostel for men.

Today it is in the process of being refurbished as business premises.

After investigating Elswick's interesting features return to the northern end of the village and slant right past Bonds Ice Cream Factory and restaurant along a narrow lane. Just before Bond's Hall Farm is reached, climb over a stile on the left bearing half right across the field passing right of a pond.

Go through a small iron gate continuing across a long narrow strip to mount a stile at the far side. Aim for the far corner of the next field to locate a hidden stile. Accompany the fence on your left to the far end of the field where a rotting footbridge is crossed. Bear right across the next field making for a stile located between two wooded ponds. From here, keep the hedge on your right to reach Watery Gate Lane through a gate.

Head left, crossing straight over at Lane Heads, to reach a junction at Manor House Farm. Keep ahead, passing through a stile at the end. Cross the field to a gate on top of an embankment. Continue onward to mount a significant flood control banking to head left. After crossing the A586, stiled at each side, another 100 metres will find us joining the embankment constructed to prevent flooding by the River Wyre.

Head left downstream keeping on the top of the embankment and accompanying the river around a sweeping left hand meander. We leave the placid waters of the river just before reaching Cartford Bridge, the only road crossing since St Michael's.

> The hotel on this side of the river of the same name is reputed to have a resident ghost which switches lights on and moves things around. Like many of the small communities in the area, it was a haven for Quaker worship at a time when non-conformists were being persecuted.

Watch for a stile in the hedge on your left as the hotel car park is neared. Cross a field to a footbridge at the far side. Then aim for the opposite corner of the next field where a gate opens onto Butt's Lane. A stroll up this hedged grassy lane will bring you to the busy main road. Great care should obviously be exercised in crossing to the far side back into Great Eccleston.

A major ghost at St Michael's

Should water cease to flow and ivy turn black, beware!

Distance: 8 miles

Height: Insignificant

Start/finish: The parish car park adjoining the primary school on Hall Lane

Terrain: Level fields surrounded by fences and hedges characterise The Fylde with many footpaths that are indistinct

Explorer 296 *Lancaster and Morecambe*

Shops etc.: St Michael's-on-Wyre

Prelude

Any walk that takes in a landscape that is as flat as the proverbial pancake cannot be recommended when mist and rain blanket the area. Save it for a fine day when the sun has got his hat on. Featureless and lacking the excitement of upland terrain, these footpaths rarely witness the passage of other walkers. That in itself should be a great attraction for those who prefer their own company.

A number of appealing villages lie scattered across this vast tract. One of the most intriguing is St Michael's. Clustered around its seventh-century church at a fording point on the River Wyre, it became a renowned tourist spot well before the days of package holidays. Visitors would 'take tea' in the many teashops that lined the main road after a stroll along the river bank.

A visit to the church will reveal a plaque on its inner wall in commemoration of those who lost their lives at the Abbeystead disaster of 1984. In all 16 villagers perished, one of whom was the husband of

St Michael's Church where a troublesome ghost was once exorcised.

Pat Seed. It was her appeal fund that raised of £3 million for cancer research.

The strangest story, however, concerns a certain Major Longworth who haunted the original St Michael's Hall nearby. A veteran of the Civil War, he was often seen parading about and caused such a furore that a priest had to be summoned to exorcise the troubled spirit. The ghost was supposedly laid to rest in a hollow beside the road bridge 'so long as the water flows down the hills and the ivy remains green'.

The Walk

Pass through a stile on the north side of the bridge heading down the river Wyre past a pair of fishing ponds. Immediately beyond these after the stile, make a half right crossing of the open field to reach

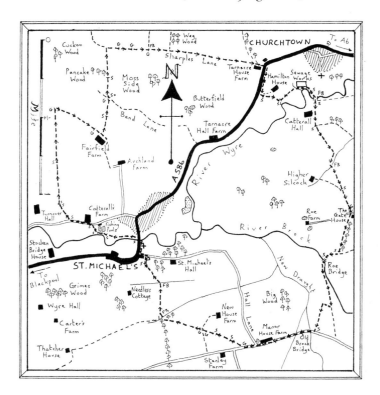

Rawcliffe Road by means of another stile. Bear left for 100 metres then mount a stile on the far side crossing a field to a stile in the hedge. Go left over another to head due north on the left side of a fenced enclosure.

Many of the fields hereabouts are separated by drainage ditches, far more useful than mere fences on this type of land. At the end of this field watch for a hidden stile in the fence. Continue onward as far as a gate and the start of a clear field track breaking right.

After passing through a gate and opposite Fairfield Farm, bear left across a field to a stile in the hedge at the far side. Keep onward to a gate at the end of the next field and a track called Band Lane. Step over a wire fence to continue heading due north. Straddle a stile on the right side of the appropriately titled Pancake Wood, keeping alongside the hedge to reach Sharples Lane.

Initially overgrown, this hedged track heads due east. After negotiating four gates to reach Moss Side Farm, keep heading due east for another half mile to reach the main A586 just after Tarnacre House Farm. Loud noises in the vicinity are caused by the local clay pigeon shooting club.

Bear right for 300 metres to join the entrance drive for Hamilton House Farm. A stile on the right offers a detour from the original right-of-way. Circle the field up to a double stile. Keep alongside a hedge beyond the farm to reach a footbridge over a small brook. A narrow path leads round past the sewage works and along the Wyre up to the substantial footbridge over to Catterall Hall.

> *If time permits, a visit to Churchtown over to the left is heartily recommended. If St Michael's is the 'Jewel of The Fylde', the St Helens at Churchtown is the 'Cathedral'. Now by-passed by the main road, the village is not on the tourist itinerary so people miss out on a true gem complete with its original preaching cross.*

After crossing the splendid suspension bridge, head south along the Hall access road until it swings sharp left. Continue straight on, heading south through a gap stile and along a hedge to the field end. Bear right here to locate a footbridge then south again until a stile gives onto the access road serving Higher Silcock. Go straight over a crossroads and through a gate to swing right at The Gate House.

A stile gives onto an overgrown path that accompanies a narrow strip of woodland. Emerge at the end over another stile slanting right to accompany an embankment for 100 metres round to Roe Bridge. At the far side of the River Brock keep to the embankment for 100 metres, then fork right away from the river along a clear track.

This leads directly to the Myerscough road, although the true path veers right at the first fence then across to a stile close to Old Brock Bridge. Head right along the road keeping straight ahead when it heaves right just after Manor House Farm.

Old cottages lying the main street in St Michael's-on-Wyre.

Watch for a signpost and gate after 200 metres. Stick with the hedge on your left over two stiles to reach a farm track gated at either side. Keep onward to pass through a small wood with footbridge and gate at the far side. Bear across to the hedge and accompany it due north for a quarter mile up to another footbridge. After trundling across this, make a half left diagonal crossing back to the edge of St Michael's. Locate a hedged gap to reach the car park through a stiled passageway adjacent to the primary school.

Tragedy at Fairhurst

A macabre story mingles effortlessly within this natural wonderland

Distance: 4.5 miles
Height: 150 feet (46 metres)

Start/finish: Between the Brock Valley and Inglewhite lies
the dispersed hamlet of Fairhurst. Ample parking is available
on the grass verge immediately to the east of the farm

Terrain: Enclosed rolling meadows in the shadow of
Beacon Fell split by the tree-fringed River Brock. Away
from the river, much of the route is pathless

Outdoor leisure 41 *Forest of Bowland*

Shops etc.: Catterall

Prelude

*The foothills on the south-west fringe of the Bowland Fells comprise
a green patchwork of fields and scattered farmsteads. Divided by a
network of narrow lanes, it is easy to lose one's sense of direction
amidst the grassy pastures. Unlike the rich cultivation characteristic
of the South Lancashire Plain, this landscape affords an exclusive preserve upon which sheep and cattle are able to graze undisturbed.*

*Of the isolated settlements, the cluster of stone cottages that com-
prise Higher Fairhurst just to the north of Inglewhite is infamous for
a tragic sequence of events where the grim reaper took a heavy toll.
Unlike the idyllic nirvana that is presented to the modern world, life in
early Victorian Lancashire could be desperate for the rural poor.*

*One such family were the Sandersons. Originally from Lancaster,
where the husband ran a butcher's shop, they moved here when the
business failed. A second shop also began to lose money, forcing the
husband to obtain a labouring job to help pay off their debts.*

His wife Ann became ever more depressed, at one point leaving her family to reside with a brother in Manchester. After two months she returned and life appeared to continue as usual. But in September 1838 a passing farmer was summoned by Mrs Sanderson who was extremely distressed that all five of her children had been struck down by food poisoning.

The local doctor duly arrived and offered a slice of a suspect pudding to a duck, which immediately fell ill and died. Within a few hours, all of the children had similarly passed away. So mortified was Ann Sanderson at this tragic turn of events that she sent for the local priest to purge her soul. Just prior to her own passage into the next world, she confessed that increasing debt and severe depression had led her to put arsenic in the food.

The inquest held at the Green Man in Inglewhite ruled that the poor woman had suffered from 'temporary insanity'. The infamy of the case was such that hoards of gaping onlookers poured in to Goosnargh to attend the funeral. Led by the priest and grief-stricken husband, the cortege finally reached the cemetery, but the coffins were unable to be finally consigned to their graves until late that night when the crowds had dispersed.

Our walk begins at Fairhurst where murder was once committed.

The Walk

Walking between the buildings of Higher Fairhurst, you will emerge at the rear into a field. Head due north along a broad hedged corridor mounting a stile midway until a gate bars further progress. Slip to the right of this and over a fence stile to continue ahead, but bear to the left past a rough depression lined with gorse bushes. At the far side, a plank footbridge and stile allow onward progress, this time bearing half right.

Fork into the fence on the right to surmount another stile and footbridge, then over the next field maintaining a straight course and heading generally north east. On your right is the dome of Lower Trotter Hill so named because horses were once exercised here prior to being sold.

Straddle a fence stile to amble alongside the hedge on your left as far as a pond. To its left another stile deposits you in the adjoining field, there to bear half right making a diagonal crossing to the far left corner to reach back lane by means of another stile.

Head right for a quarter mile taking note of an unusual feature in this part of the world – a thatched cottage called Higher Stanalee. Just beyond a T-junction, heave a left through a gate heading north once again. After passing the small wood on the right, keep to the fence to the end of the field marked by a tree-lined gully.

Cross the fence stile and over the next field to another with an accompanying plank footbridge. Immediately to the west rises the distinctive dome of Beacon Fell Country Park.

> *Originally named 'Threlfall Beacon' after a local family, it offers nature trails ensconced within a proud wig of conifers.*

> *Much of the land hereabouts was owned by the Knights of St John of Jerusalem in medieval times. This monastic order had a religious as well as military role, diligently protecting the Cross whilst following a life of poverty and chastity.*

When the fence veers away to the right, keep a direct course steering left of a fenced enclosure to join White Lee Lane via a stile. Then

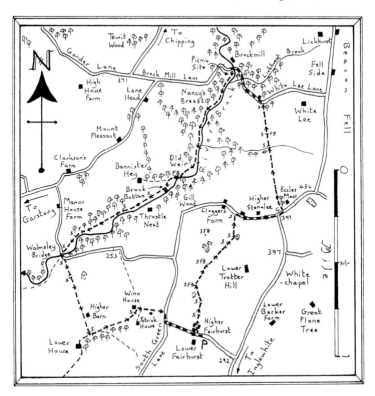

bear left down into the confines of the Brock Valley. After crossing the second bridge, swing immediately left along the riverside at Brock Mill picnic site and car park.

This was the site of a large water-powered corn mill, many of the grindstones ending up in nearby gardens. Look out for the unusual Badger carvings.

The clear path sticks closely to the chattering river as it bustles downstream to merge with the River Wyre at St Michaels. This section, amidst dense tree cover, is an utter delight and should not in any circumstances be rushed. Carry on until a broken weir is reached,

Remains of Brock Bottom Mill hidden among the trees.

at which point the path trails away from the river for a short distance, traversing open ground until a footbridge is reached.

Keep to this side of the river for a further 100 metres until the path divides. Take the left branch but watch for a narrow passage soon passing right of the ruined Brock Bottom Mill. A decaying shell cloaked in ivy, it was once a thriving industry powered by water from the river.

Continue along the riverbank crossing a fence stile and open grassland with a line of trees set back on the right. A short wooded sector, stiled at each end, will then find you approaching Walmsley Bridge where we leave the river trail to head left for no more than 50 metres.

Mount a stile on the far side of the lane to cross a field to a stile at the opposite side. Keep a straight course across a large open field parallel with overhead power lines on the right to arrive at a gate. The track now funnels into a hedged corridor. Wander past Higher Barn down to a T-junction. Swing left, mounting the stile on the left, to follow an enclosed woodland walkway. A thin path indicates this is rarely used. It is likely to be a little soft in midcourse, especially after rain.

Arriving at Winn House, mount a stile then swing right down the access track to Join South Green Lane. Make a right followed soon after by a left for the return to Higher Fairhurst.

Don't cross the green man

Being a focus of post endeavour has served to enhance Inglewhite's appeal

Distance: 5.5 miles
Height: 100 feet (30 metres)

Start/finish: Ample parking is available on the roadside opposite the Green Man Hotel in Inglewhite

Terrain: Rolling pastures rise gradually from the flatness of the Fylde to merge into the bleak uplands of the Bowland Fells

Explorer OL41 *Forest of Bowland*, and Explorer 286 *Preston and Blackburn*

Shops etc.: Inglewhite

Prelude

A maze of hedged fields interspersed with narrow lanes characterises the foothills lying in the shadow of the Bowland Fells. Most visitors have a tendency to aim for Beacon Fell Country Park. Yet the surrounding countryside offers fine rambling terrain incorporating many unusual features. Inglewhite is one such gem. Quaint, alluring, attractive and engaging; there are a host of such clichés that we can apply to a village which has lost none of its fascination over the years.

Modern commercialisation has thankfully failed to dent its ancient allure. The market cross dominates the split village green where roads from the four points of the compass converge. This was one of the main reasons for the village's importance in days of yore. Over ten feet high, the mounting stone is inscribed with the appendage 'HCIW. 1675' and relates to Justice Warren who was Lord of the Manor.

At this time, tolls were collected for the passage of vehicles and animals along the road through the village – 2½ old pence for a cow and the same for twenty sheep. The Green Man was used for

The Green Man at Inglewhite where the trial of Ann Sanderson took place
(Walk 20).

conducting legal proceedings and included the coroner's court when unusual deaths were investigated.

Just south of the pub is the congregational chapel erected in 1826 on the site of the old chucking pit, which was the site of a primitive method of giving judgement on alleged witches. A bizarre practice, it supposedly proved that those who sank must be guilty.

A fine array of stone farms and cottages lines the green, which once hosted an important agricultural fair where many of the local products were sold. Button Street and Silk Mill Lane are an indication of the industries that helped make the village an important commercial focus. In the nineteenth century, the vicar of Goosnargh banned the holding of fairs on Sunday, supposedly because he objected to bull-baiting. Prior to this the health-giving properties of water from Saint Anne's Well attracted many partakers.

The Walk

Our walk begins from the village green by heading north west through a farmyard on the left. Stroll down a fenced corridor along

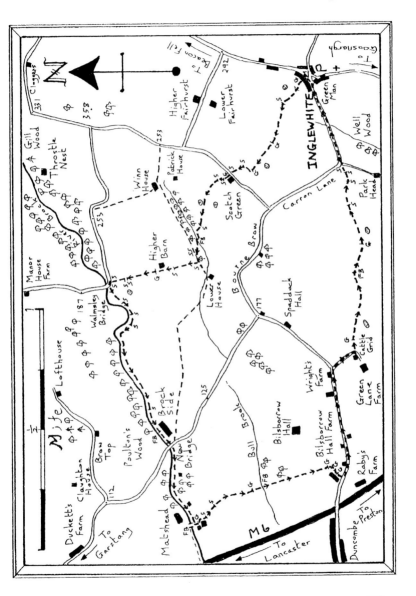

to the first stile. Now accompany the hedge on your left to the end of the field, passing into the adjacent field to continue on the opposite side up to a fence. Go through the gate and along to a stile, making a half right crossing of this field to reach South Green Lane.

Go straight over the road and through the access gate serving Scotch Green. Mount a ladder stile on the right bearing left to skirt the buildings to a stile beyond. Now keep the hedge on your right all the way to the stretch of woodland ahead. Mount a stile leaning hard left to drop down into a glen crossing a footbridge below. Climb up the facing brief slope to emerge from the woods at the far side by means of a double stile.

Head left to join the access track of Lower House, but swing right to pass High Barn heading onward to pass through a gate at the end. This section of the walk to Walmsley Bridge is covered in the opposite direction on Walk 20. Stay parallel to the overhead power lines on your left all the way to Walmsley Bridge, straddling a double stile part way.

Now bear left following a clear field track along the wooded course of the River Brock all the way downstream to Brock Side. Numerous fence stiles are surmounted *en route*. Keep an eye open for the caperings of wild deer that live in the wooded tract on the far side of the river. The path funnels into a fenced passage squeezed between stone residences and the river.

Emerging onto a back lane beside New Bridge, cross straight over to accompany a partly paved track to its end near to a footbridge spanning the River Brock. Ignore this to swing hard left into the yard of a private house, keeping left of the out-buildings. Watch for a narrow gate in the fence opposite that will be a struggle for those of stout proportions, or like me, with wide rucksacks.

Keep left across a stretch of lawn to mount a stile depositing you in the field behind. Cross to a stile on the far side in a hedge. Head south alongside the hedge on your right, passing through a gate at the end. Another 100 metres will see you crossing a footbridge to join a paved field road that leads unerringly to Bilsborough Hall Farm.

Inglewhite was once an important focus of industry.

After passing through the initial two gates, keep left through another into a field. Bear right along the back of a byre returning to the farm proper through another. Head left round the outbuildings to gain the farm access road and so on to join the Bilsborough/Inglewhite road.

Head left for a half mile then right down the access road for Green Lane Farm. At the cattle grid, bear left along a hedged corridor passing through a gate at the end. Heading due east with the hedge on your right, cross a footbridge to reach a gate. Avoid an obvious field track, instead leaning half left up to the far corner of the field.

Once over the stile, follow the hedge on your left to a stile at the end veering left over two more to rejoin the main road. It is then but a short stroll up the road back into Inglewhite.

Tottering along the ridge

The desolate moors of the Bowland Fells offer high level walking of the highest order

Distance: 8.5 miles
Summit: Totridge 1,627 feet
Height: 1,100 feet (335 metres)

Start/finish: Ample roadside parking at the entrance to the Langden Valley two miles west of Dunsop Bridge

Terrain: Deeply cut valleys with steep sides give way to rough heather and peat moorland

Explorer OL41 *Forest of Bowland*

Shops etc.: Dunsop Bridge

Prelude

Often ignored by walkers, the Bowland Fells offer lonely and exhilarating hikes for the discerning few. More akin to Pennine terrain, these desolate moors lack the bold assertiveness of Lakeland; nor do they equate to the limestone cragginess of the Yorkshire Dales. And nowhere do the rolling gritstone uplands exceed the magical contour of 2,000 feet. But what they lack in stature and an aggressive 'in your face' attitude is more than made up for by a penetrating sense of isolation and remoteness.

Broad swathes of heather and peat bog with a few identifiable landmarks ensure that this feeling is no brief illusion. Once the valleys are left behind, the solitary walker is indeed on his own, remote from civilisation and dependent on his own resources.

Paths are few in number, confined to key access points. This is because much of the area is restricted by private ownership. It is to be hoped that, in the near future, the 'right to roam' movement will be successful in achieving a much wider public access.

Bowland is the eleventh largest Area of Outstanding Natural Beauty

in the country. It is a protected heritage site with the local authority working in co-operation with landowners, farmers and the local communities. A ten-year plan hopes to build on past achievements and develop new opportunities where recreation and conservation go hand in hand.

The Walk

At Langden Brook where our walk begins, North West Water are channelling the catchment area to improve the water supply in the Ribble Valley. Stroll up the access road to the pumping station circling right past a small reservoir. Beyond a stile, a wide track used

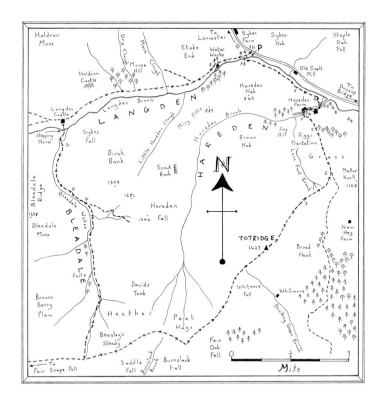

119

by excavation vehicles heads up valley. When this veers away up the right flank fork left along a lower trail, though still above the level flood plain, of the meandering brook.

Steep slopes of rough grass shoot up on either side with numerous cuttings known as cloughs channelling water into the main brook. After two miles, the track angles down to valley level at Langden Castle.

Only a huddle of dark stones remains of the original structure which has been replaced by a heavily secured new building. At either side, an open niche provides shelter from inclement weather.

Our way lies due south along the side valley of Bleadale. Look for a loose set of stepping stones to cross Langden Brook. Add a few of

A new building occupies the site of the enigmatic Langden Castle.

your own to build up this crossing point which can be tricky when the stream is in spate. Crossing to the left side of Bleadale Water needs to be done where it narrows at the right of two meanders. Now climb above the valley bottom to pass through a fence gate.

A clear path opens up leading into the constricted body of Bleadale itself. This trail is a delight to follow, increasing in interest as time passes. At a tight section, pass through two gates after which the path divides. Ignore the obvious trail winding up the hillside on your left. Stick to the valley trail which soon begins to climb through heather as the source of the beck is approached.

Constricted views lend an air of eerie remoteness to this hidden valley. As height is gained, our route lies to the right crossing numerous rills but still maintaining a southerly direction. Eventually, we climb out onto the open heather moor above. Follow a thin path in the heather keeping a set of marker posts in sight. Crossing a featureless tract for a quarter mile, these will lead you to the east-west fence that traverses the undulating plateau.

A bleak and inhospitable scene now unfolds. This is definitely not the sort of place to opt for a broken leg. Head left along the fence surmounting numerous peat hags round to an abrupt corner on Fair Oak Fell. The difficult nature of the terrain with no visible landmarks makes this section appear much longer than the map would indicate. At the fence corner, bear left sticking to the fence between the unending series of peat hags.

When the fence veers away to the right, keep onward to join a wall. As the crest of the ridge is neared, the path forks away left onto the summit of Totridge with its white trig column. Maintain a north easterly bearing down the long ridge to meet up with the wall below. Accompany it down a steep grass bank to mount a stile thereafter continuing downhill with a fence on your right. In the depression, cross the splayed source rills of Lane Foot Brook ambling up the far side for a short distance only.

Slant left to locate a stile in the facing wall. Then stroll down the smooth grass slope to straddle another stile at the bottom with Riggs Plantation on the right. Continue down to the valley road and the

Summit of Totridge surrounded by endless peat moorland.

farming hamlet of Hareden. After crossing the bridge, bear right past the old farmhouse which was built in 1690.

A hundred metres before reaching the main Trough of Bowland road, slant left over a stone bridge then right to locate a wall stile close to Langden Brook. Head left upstream meeting a wall stile after 300 metres. The permissive path keeps parallel to the watercourse heading back towards the entrance to the Langden Valley. Cross a footbridge and stile to rejoin the outward access road.

All's fair on the snape

A heady mix of high level fell wandering and ancient ancestry

Distance: 8 miles
Summits: Parlick 1,417 feet. Fair Snape Fell 1,673 feet
Height: 1,200 feet (366 metres)

Terrain: Wild untainted moorland, mainly grass but with extensive peat hags

Start/finish: Ample roadside parking available along the road which terminates at Fell Foot

Explorer L41 *Forest of Bowland*

Shops etc.: Chipping

Prelude

Standing aloof from the more popular regions of Northern England, the Bowland Fells have been designated an Area of Outstanding Natural Beauty since 1964. This has effectively protected them from any form of unwelcome exploitation. Although surrounded by busy roads, this unique landscape of windswept moorland still remains largely unknown to the majority of walkers.

This is perhaps due to much of the area being held in private ownership with only limited access being allowed to ramblers. The establishment of a 'right to roam' which has caused much friction over the years is now coming to fruition. It is therefore hoped that far more land will soon become available for responsible walkers to enjoy, and any problems this may cause will be amicably resolved to everyone's satisfaction.

At the present time, walkers are presented with a vast array of byel-aws displayed on prominent signs when entering these 'access' areas. And it goes without saying that you will diligently read every one of them prior to setting off.

Often referred to as the Forest of Bowland, the upper slopes remain

as bald as the legendary coot. This impressive title alludes to the area being a royal preserve for the hunting of deer in medieval times. There can be no denying that Bowland is a wild and remote place with few tracks and vast acres that never see a human soul from one year to the next. Even on the edge you are more likely to have the fells to yourself, except that is for the paragliders who use the eastern slopes of Parlick for take-offs.

The Walk

Indeed, as you stroll up the road to the renovated cottage of Fell Foot, a small wind sock provides flyers with the direction of blow. Go through the gate to head straight up the fell beside a water cut gully, keeping straight ahead when the path leans to the right. This is the only steep part of the whole walk and is soon over as the stony summit of Parlick hoves into view.

Our main objective, Fair Snape Fell, lies across the side valley of the infant River Brock. Cross to the opposite side of the fence by

Fair Snape Fell seen from the summit of Parlick.

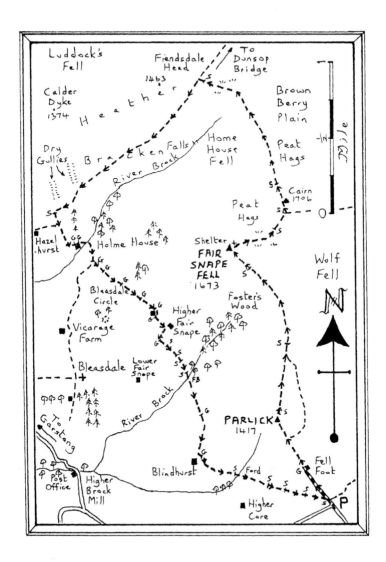

Summit cairn and shelter on Fair Snape Fell.

a ladder stile taking the precaution of concealing any dogs in your rucksack. Our canine companions are not welcome in the 'access areas'. Follow the fence down into a depression and up the far side straddling a fence stile before leaning away from the fell wall. An easy gradient follows across rising ground over one more fence stile before the summit of the main fell is reached.

The broad plateau affords a far-reaching panorama across the Fylde. Our way heads east along a thin path that soon picks a way over the never-ending sea of peat hags, an ocean of hummocky green reassembling sea elephants at rest. After joining a fence, a stile is mounted soon after. Keep the main fence on your right for a further 300 metres whence another stile is crossed.

Bear away left after this leaving the east-bound fence to head downhill with another fence on your left. As height is lost, this section becomes rather messy and a little hard on the ankles. On reaching Fiendsdale Head, mount the fence stile to head south west along a path that improves as height is lost. Heathery moor gives way to bracken-cloaked slopes as the path veers down to meet the first in-take wall.

Stick with this until opposite the second of two dry gullies then swing left over a stile and down to meet the access track serving Home House. Go through the farmyard by two gates leaning right thereafter.

Just beyond the next gate, our route leaves the main track forking left alongside a fence. Now heading south east, you should pass through four gates to reach an isolated barn. Another gate beyond will find you approaching the farming hamlet of Higher Fair Snape. Go down the access track and take a look over to a clump of trees lying a quarter mile to the west.

Ensconced within is the celebrated Bleasdale Circle. A Bronze Age relic from around 800 BC, it was discovered in 1898. Like all such artefacts, its origins are steeped in mystery. In the beginning there were two circles, one inside the other. The larger was very unusual being composed of oak posts.

One of only three in Europe that are made of wooden columns, the others are near Stonehenge in Wiltshire and Cologne in Germany. The posts were thoughtlessly ripped out and replaced by concrete, thus spoiling the site forever. The original remains are housed in the Harris Museum at Preston, which is the nearest you will come to viewing the circle as it is on private land.

So head left after 50 metres through a gate along a path with a fence on your left. Go through another gate after 300 metres then watch for a fence stile to deposit you in the adjoining field on the left. Continue down to mount a fence stile and cross the River Brock by a footbridge. Then head out of the tree cover across to the far corner of the field where fences converge where we pass through a gate.

Here we join a major field track to ford a tributary of the Brock continuing onward to the farm of Blindhurst. Do not enter the yard. Instead, bear left through a gate and then around to the right to slant across the lower slopes of Parlick, climbing gradually to the top corner. Choose the second stile to ford another stream in a deep cutting.

Maintain a level course keeping parallel to the in-take wall on the left to reach the next wall stile. Another follows after a further 150 metres. Keep above the line of trees crossing a small beck bearing away left to the next wall stile. The final stroll is down a shallow grade aiming for the far corner of the field to reach the Fell Foot road.

Ribbed by the Romans

An ancient pedigree of both Roman and Norman vintage makes for an interesting foray

Distance: 6 miles
Height: 350 feet (107 metres)

Start/finish: Make use of the large free car park on the west side of Ribchester

Terrain: Grassy slopes rise gradually from the river that gives the village its name.
Paths are indistinct for much of the route

Explorer 19 *West Pennine Moors*

Shops etc.: Ribchester

Prelude

Even if the narrow streets of Ribchester are bursting at the seams with visitors, you will be assured of seclusion on this walk. This really is a splendid circuit around a site of antiquity that the early Romans knew so well. Before setting out, stroll down the main street, paying special attention to the White Bull with its Roman columns taken from the original Bremetennacum fort.

This strategic base was erected where the arrow-straight highway linking Manchester with Hadrian's Wall crossed the Ribble Valley. The Roman invaders were astute enough to realise that this was the best place for a crossing and future settlement. Today only scattered remnants of this proud lineage can be traced, some in the vicinity of St Wilfred's Church. The Romans must have been an extremely hygienic people as the Bath House is the main surviving relic of their occupation. The museum offers a feast of information about the village's noble heritage.

At the bottom of the road, it becomes clear why Ribchester's popularity has reached beyond its historical traditions. In more recent times,

Visit the Roman bath house in Ribchester.

weaving was a major source of work and many of the older houses had hand looms in their back rooms.

Following a wander round Ribchester, head down to the riverside. Being the only village actually located along the banks of the Ribble is an obvious attraction as the line of memorial seats testify.

The Walk

Our walk begins from here by heading left upstream for 100 metres before an abrupt left in the tree cover brings you to the Bath House site. Retrace your steps continuing along the road, taking the path that circles round the edge of the churchyard with a kissing gate at either end. St Wilfred's dates from the thirteenth century and is built on the site of a pre-Norman church.

Head left along the access road serving Parsonage Farm leaving this just before a sharp kink to mount the stile on the right. Circle round

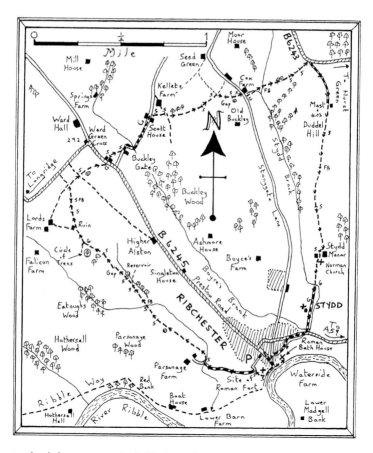

to the left, up a gentle field slope, keeping parallel to a hedge 100 metres on the left. On meeting a hedge at the top end, stay right of it for 150 metres to mount a stile, thereafter dropping down to cross a stream by a stile/footbridge.

Mount the facing slope above a tree-lined tributary until a stile can be mounted. Do not follow the obvious track. Instead fork left over a fence stile into a narrow fenced corridor until a gap on the left enables you to continue a north westerly direction in the field proper.

At the end, straddle a stile and fork left over to the opposite corner passing to the right of an unusual ring of trees midway. A gate opens onto a major track.

Accompany this up to a ruin on the right. Behind this the field is crossed to its left-hand corner where a stiled footbridge is surmounted. Keep the next fence on your left over another stile, then veer away right past a pond to reach Preston Road through a gate. On the far side, slightly offset to the left, walk down the farm drive to mount a stile. Thereafter drop down to the bottom right corner of the field behind where a stile will deposit you on Green Moor Lane.

Head left up this lane for a quarter mile until you reach Scott House on the right. Inside the front entrance, bear left over a lawn and stile to cross rough ground to the stile at the far side. Join a track heading right for only 20 metres before slanting left past a line of trees. Fork away right to the far end of the field and a stile.

Accompanying the hedge on your right, stroll onward to the next stile after which bear half right over to a hedge gap. Continue over the next field to a stile hidden amidst a thick hedge on the far side. Crossing the next field will bring you to Cox Farm via a stile opening onto Stonygate Lane.

Go through a gate to the right of the farm and down the slope to cross a narrow rill by a footbridge. This stream feeds into Stydd Brook soon after. Mount the grass slope beyond to cross a field passing between an intermittent line of trees. Make your way over to a stile in the facing hedge, then aim to the right of a pond where a fence stile is straddled. Continue ahead to the B6243 at Dean Brow.

Bear right along the paved access road serving the farm on Duddel Hill. Once you have passed through the gate to the right of the buildings, go down the far side of the hill heading due south and taking advantage of a groove that will bring you to a fence stile.

Keep heading south down towards the valley bottom, the next obstruction being a hedge with footbridge. With the hedge on your right, continue downhill to cross a stile so depositing you in the adjacent field. Stick to a clear field track that will take you down to cross a stile into the farmyard of Stydd Manor.

The old Norman chapel at Stydd.

Just south of here is the isolated Norman chapel that is thought to have been a hospital managed by the Knights Hospitaller of St John of Jerusalem. Many of the old herbs used for healing the sick can still be found in the vicinity. Unchanged over centuries, this ancient throwback to the beginning of the last millennium remains largely unknown to the majority of visitors to Ribchester.

Continue past the chapel to join a paved road serving the hamlet of Stydd. On your right are the almshouses built by the Shireburnes in 1726 and which still provide homes to Catholic ladies of the parish. The entrance pillars are supposed to have been brought from the old Roman Fort. At the end of the road turn right back into Ribchester branching left along Greenside to reach Water Street.

A royal guest at the inn

*Intrigue and skulduggery provide a piquant
dessert to this Ribblesdale ramble*

Distance: 4.5 miles
Height: 350 feet (107 metres)

Start/finish: Ample parking space at a pull-in off the B6243
Longridge Road 200 metres west of the Punch Bowl
approaching Hurst Green

Terrain: Enclosed grazing fields rise gradually
from the floor of the Ribble Valley

Explorer 19 *West Pennine Moors*

Shops etc.: Hurst Green in the Ribble Valley

Prelude

*A walk of 200 metres along the B6243 in an easterly direction will
bring you to an old coaching inn called The Punch Bowl. In the early
eighteenth century, this site became the headquarters of a notorious
highwayman who preyed on unsuspecting travellers using this lonely
stretch of the Ribble Valley. Ned King and his cronies would keep
watch from a room above the stables selecting only the wealthiest
victims to waylay and rob.*

*So successful was Lancashire's answer to Dick Turpin that he
was known as 'The Phantom' on account of his ability to disappear following one of his robberies. But no highwayman can escape
indefinitely from being brought to account for his nefarious deeds.
And so it was with Ned King. Dogged perseverance eventually enabled the authorities to discover Ned's secret hideout.*

Suspicion also fell on the landlord who, they thought, was sharing in the profits of Ned's nefarious escapades. When finally arrested and brought to trial, Ned King was found guilty and his body was hung in chains from a gibbet erected in nearby Gallows Lane.

His ghost was often heard and seen in the vicinity of the Punch Bowl which resulted in an exorcism being performed in the nineteenth century. But still he continued to haunt the pub. Bottles fell off shelves, beer pumps opened and chairs clattered over. Not until 1942 when a priest was summoned from Stonyhurst College to attempt once again the eradication of this troublesome spirit did Ned King finally disappear, hopefully this time for ever. Unless, of course, you know better.

The Walk

After passing the Punch Bowl, take a left after 50 metres through a gate to stroll up the access track serving Bailey House. Keep right through the farmyard. Then make a diagonal crossing of the field behind aiming to the left of a prominent copse on Doe Hill. As a fence is approached, bear left to a stile. Once in the adjacent field follow the fence on the right to reach the left side of a wood straddling a footbridge *en route*.

Ned King hid out at the Punch Bowl.

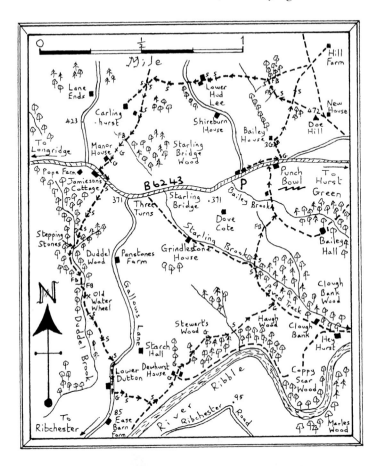

Another footbridge followed by a stile will find you striding out west over a wide field. Keep above Shireburn House seen at the far side to reach Lower Hud Lee Farm, initially hidden from view. Mount the stile then amble down the fenced passage through the farmyard to cross straight over a narrow lane.

Follow the fence on your left to a corner where a stile gives onto the adjoining field. After 50 metres, a double stile will find you crossing a grass tract, veering away from a major track leading down to Carlinghurst which is 50 metres to the right.

Keep in a direct line going downhill staying to the right of Starling Bridge Wood. You should reach the end of the field where a stile is mounted. Pass left of a newish barn and down to the far right corner to cross an old footbridge. Accompany the fence on your right in a direct line passing through two gates to reach the B6243 opposite Jamieson's Cottages.

Bear left for 100 metres, squeezing through the hedge on the far side to make a half left crossing of the field. A hedge will see you approaching the tree-lined glen of Duddel Brook. Mount the stile and follow this eastern limit of the glen before entering the dense tree cover by a stile 300 metres further down.

Stepping stones will deposit you on the far side of the stream where either the lower or higher level paths can be taken downstream. Either choices will find you crossing two footbridges to gain the opposite bank after which an old waterwheel housing is passed.

Exit the wood by a stile and follow a raised causeway down, mounting a stile midway to join Gallows Lane in the corner of the field. Continue downhill to pass the picturesque cottages of Lower Dutton nudging through a gate on the left. Stay on the left side of a hedge accompanying it round to the right after 100 metres to mount a stile.

Now on the right of the hedge, follow it down to mount a stile at the end and so joining the Ribble Way, a long-distance footpath that chaperones the river all the way down to the Irish Sea beyond Preston. Head left upstream along a paved road that leads into the yard of Dewhurst House. The Way bears right to follow the river to its source at Ribblehead in the Yorkshire Dales.

Here we leave the Way slanting right through a small gate and up a narrow hedged passage which is stony underfoot. Emerging onto higher ground by a gate, follow a set of white marker posts that provide an easy linkage across this section of the walk. Go through a gate at the top edge of Stewart's Wood forking away left when the fence veers down towards the river.

The picturesque setting of Lower Dutton.

Descend an easy grass slope to a stile and fieldbridge crossing of a stream flowing through Haugh Wood. Climb up the bank on the far side and make a direct crossing of the large field to a gate at the far right corner. Bear left along a paved bridleway for a quarter mile until a stile gives access to the trees enclosing Starling Brook. Drop down through the trees traversing the brook by a footbridge.

Another stile at the far side of the wood will find you crossing a field to bestride another footbridge on the left. Continue onward to meet the service road for Bailey Hall and follow it left back to the main road near to the Punch Bowl. And perchance a noggin or two with the spirit of Ned King to finish off this fine ramble.

This green and pleasant land

Enjoy a walk where educational endeavour flirts with mysterious intrigue

Distance: 3.5 miles
Height: 300 feet (91 metres)

Start/finish: Parking presents no problems in the centre of Hurst Green near the village cross

Terrain: Rolling farmland drops sharply to the flat terrace of the River Ribble which swings across the valley in a series of wide loops

Explorer 19 *West Pennine Moors*

Shops etc.: Hurst Green

Prelude

Hurst Green is a proud village, not least because for two years running in 1992/93 it was voted the best kept small village in Lancashire. A pair of circular plaques mounted on stone are displayed beside the village green for all to see. They stand adjacent to a pair of crosses that also proclaim an impressive pedigree, showing that Hurst Green is rightly a village in which locals can be well satisfied.

Following the closure of two weaving mills which complemented the farming traditions in the area, tourists began to recognise the endearing qualities of Hurst Green. They arrived by means of a ferry service over the river before Dinckley Bridge was constructed. It remains a popular destination to this day with many visitors calling at the Shireburn, a hotel named after the village's seventeenth-century benefactor.

Richard Shireburn erected some almshouses in 1706 on Keppel End, but these were later systematically removed to their present location at

WALK 26

138

Hurst Green displays its award-winning plaques with pride.

the edge of the village to house workers at Stonyhurst College. It was this magnificent structure that commenced its life as the family home of the Shireburns.

The Walk

From the village green, stroll down Warren Fold beside the cross, which in summer is a mass of colour ensconced within a flowering bonanza. At the end of the short cul-de-sac, continue ahead over a number of stiles with a stone wall on your left until you reach the hedge abutting the primary school.

Bear right along this to the field corner where another path is joined heading right towards Stonyhurst College. The domed towers poking above the tree tops of Fox Fell Wood indicate our immediate objectives. Pass through two kissing gates before crossing a shallow depression thereafter nudging the wood on you left.

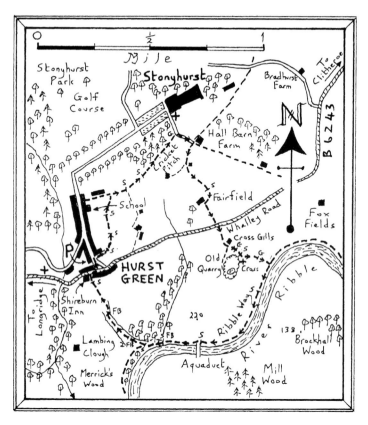

The path forges onward along a broad corridor with a fence on the right. At the far end, negotiate a gate to join a side road for the brief stroll to the college buildings.

> *The church of St Peter, built in 1702 by the Shireburn Family, dominates the foreground. The hall fell into disuse after the youngest son died from eating yew berries, supposedly having found himself lost in the local maze.*

> *Following the demise of the Shireburn name, it passed into the hands of the Weld family. They in turn leased it to the Jesuits*

140

A strange legend inveigles this stone cross overlooking the Ribble valley.

who had moved here from France to establish a seat of learning after being persecuted by the Revolutionaries. They used the stables as a chapel before the present baronial church was constructed. The college has since developed in to a private institution of educational distinction being one of the most prestigious in the country.

During the holidays this elegantly restored mansion opens its doors to the public who can visit the unique library. One of the exhibits is the prayer book held by Mary Queen of Scots at her execution. Another fascinating item is the table where Oliver Cromwell rested during his advance on Preston in 1648. Sleeping in full armour clutching a pistol, he had no intention of being caught napping by skulking royalists. His army made do with an open camp in Stonyhurst Park.

Once this striking edifice has been admired, amble back to pass the gate continuing onward along the metalled road serving Hall Bank Farm. Bend right here beside the cricket ground. When the pavilion access track forks right, keep ahead to pass through a kissing gate and round to reach Fair Field. Slant left down the access track to cross straight over the B6243 down the track for Cross Gills.

At the far end of the farmyard keep left through a gate and down a fenced passage to mount a stile continuing down the fenced passage. Beyond a gate, watch for a prominent stone cross erected on the hill to your right. A brief climb will be rewarded by the superb panorama which opens up spanning the Ribble Valley. On the far side of the valley, the jutting prow of Pendle Hill forms an impressive backdrop to complement the strange fable that surrounds the arcane curiosity.

Ornately carved from local stone, the cross was placed here in 1830 to replace the original which had been destroyed. Legend has it that the Crosskill Family who ran the farm below perpetrated this wanton act of vandalism, but the reasoning behind their actions remains a mystery. It clearly upset somebody, for a lurid force was unleashed resulting in three members of the family dying in mystifying circumstances.

A poignant tale to mull over whilst descending the steep grass slope through a loose scattering of trees to rejoin the path. Pass through a gate alongside the hedge on your left to meet the row of trees that line the snaking twist of the Ribble. Head right downstream keeping close to the river in a wide sweep; straddle a fence stile after 200 metres.

On reaching a stone aqueduct over the water, mount a stile to pass right of the structure. Then continue onward to enter the confines of a wood by means of a footbridge followed immediately by a stile. Thereafter, the thin path climbs away from the river through the woodland to emerge into a field above. Once over the first stile beyond the upper fence, accompany another fence on your left up a ridge between two minor streams.

After 100 metres, straddle two footbridges climbing the grass bank steadily and bearing right over another footbridge to continue uphill towards Hurst Green with a hedge on your left. A low wall stile at the top end will find you arriving on the village street beside The Shireburn.

Treasure and the occult

A priceless hoard combines with mysterious collusion to mesmeric effect

Distance: 5 miles
Height: 250 feet (76 metres)

Start/finish: Park on Cooper Hill Drive 200 metres west of
St Leonard's Church on the A6230 in Walton-le-Dale

Terrain: Enclosed pastures above the valley drop quite
abruptly to the flat bottomlands on either side
of the River Ribble

Explorer 286 *Blackburn and Preston*

Shops etc.: Walton-le-Dale

Prelude

Since Saxon times the site of Walton-le-Dale had been of strategic
importance. A vital fording point before a bridge was built, it held
the key to the defence of Preston by the Royalists in the English
Civil War. They held out for three days until the might of Cromwell's
army eventually prevailed. Today, the village concentrates on market
gardening along the fertile banks of the River Darwin.

The old church has a particularly macabre past involving the 'rais-
ing of the dead' by Edward Kelley in 1560. Learning that a recently
buried man had left a lot of wealth in a secret location, Kelley exerted
occult powers to discover its whereabouts. Various incantations and
spells are said to have re-animated the corpse which then revealed all.
Whether this wealth could have been the mysterious Cuerdale Hoard
will be investigated during this walk.

Such was the esteem that purveyors of the occult enjoyed that
Kelley was knighted as a hero in Germany for his dark sorcery. He
died in 1595 after falling through a window. Clearly his powers did not
pertain to extending his life in perpetuity.

Occult spells were invoked in the graveyard of St Leonard's Church in Walton-le-Dale.

The Walk

Follow Edward Kelley's footsteps along the path that commences between the church and the old red sandstone schoolhouse. Go behind the church and along the path through the large graveyard and down a passage that emerges onto the road just past the Catholic Church of Our Lady and St Patrick.

Cross over to take a hedged path that soon traverses the River Darwin by a substantial footbridge. Bear left to amble upstream for 200 metres before the path forks away from the river. Make a gradual ascent through the trees on a disintegrating flight of worn stone steps. Once above the flood plain, head south alongside the edge of Mosney Wood entering Nook Farmyard by a gate.

Stroll down the access road until it veers right, at which point mount a fence stile continuing ahead to the far side of the field. Straddle another stile, walking along a constricted passage between sheltered housing and industrial units. Emerging onto Cottage Lane, bear left for 300 metres to cross the M6.

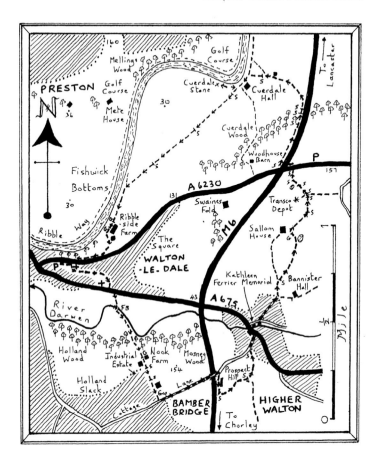

Take the first right and when the paved road ends, straddle a stile and keep following the track around to the left. Watch for an indistinct left fork after 200 metres and a stile, after which the path descends a grassy bank winging left at the bottom to rejoin Cottage Lane at the edge of Higher Walton.

Head right along a row of terraced cottages to the village centre where the Mill Tavern gives a clear indication of the settlement's industrial past. The mill itself, once used for cotton spinning, has now been broken up into small business units. Make a left at the roundabout then right immediately after crossing the River Darwin bridge. On the corner is a memorial garden to the renowned opera singer Kathleen Ferrier CBE who was born in Higher Walton.

Pass through the gate to accompany the riverbank for 100 metres, forking left up a cul-de-sac of dormer bungalows. At the end, enter a field taking the left fork until the track enters an adjacent field. Mount a stile here to following the hedge on your right past a large pond until you reach a gate at the top end.

Here, bear half right across to a stile at the far side entering a narrow hedged passage. At its end cross the access road serving the Transco Gas Depot stiled at each side. Thereafter aiming half left, go to the far side of this small field and straddle a fence stile. Then continue onward to another giving onto the A6230. Bear left over the motorway then immediately right to accompany this highway north for a half mile.

After passing the eastern stiled limit of Cuerdale Wood, drop down a grass bank to mount a double stile. Soon after make a wide left-hand sweep towards the far side of the field passing left of an isolated structure. Another 100 metres finds you mounting a fence stile for the approach to Cuerdale Hall and the low banking of the River Ribble.

Follow this downstream for 200 metres to locate the hidden site of the famed Cuerdale Hoard.

A stone column fixed in a depression indicates where this substantial cache of Viking treasure was unearthed on 15 May 1840 by a gang of workmen. Much of the silver coinage minted at York and jewellery dating from around 928 AD was concealed in a leaden chest. Declared as Treasure Trove, it was distributed to various museums apart from certain pieces that found their way into local homes. Why the treasure was buried in this obscure site has always remained a mystery that is yet to be solved. Any ideas?

Returning to the Hall, make a right soon mounting a stile to follow the hedge on your left over two more stiles until the broad meander of the Ribble is regained. Amble down a track to pass Ribble Side Farm swinging left to gain the access track which climbs out of the valley to meet the A6230. Head right down Cooper Hill back into Walton-le-Dale.

Site of the Cuerdale Hoard on the banks of the Ribble.

Beef to knight

Feasting and excess mark the origin of England's most traditional meal

Distance: 7 miles
Height: 650 feet (198 metres)

Start/finish: Leave the M65 taking the A675 to Riley Green. Bear left along A6061 then left again down Sandy Lane. After 200 metres, park on the grass verge near a barn.

Terrain: Rolling foothills to the north of the moors are cut by deep river valleys

Explorer 19 *West Pennine Moors*

Shops etc.: Hoghton

Prelude

One of the finest old houses in Lancashire has to be the ancient fortified mansion of the de Hoghton Family, appropriately named Hoghton Tower. It has been in the family since the time of William the Conqueror, although the current building only dates from the sixteenth century. Occupying a superb site on the hilltop overlooking the Derwent Valley, it is surrounded by trees and only visible from the end of the half-mile driveway.

A war memorial has been erected opposite the entrance which affords a fine view up to the battlemented façade. This drive was only built in 1901, the original commencing from the Royal Oak Hotel in Riley Green. This can still be recognised in its initial stages before blending into the enclosed field pattern.

In those far off days when lavish entertainment was expected from the landed gentry, Richard de Hoghton organised a monumental feast when the King visited in 1617. James I was so impressed by a particular joint of beer that he dubbed it 'Sir Loin'. And so it has remained to this day. The dining table where James ate is supposedly still in the

The Sirloin commemorates a famous cut of beef.

same position. It is also commemorated in the name of the local pub adjacent to the railway crossing in the village.

Financial embarrassment following the royal visit led to a period of incarceration in the debtors' prison for the unfortunate Richard. One neighbour is said to have burned his house down rather than succumb to such pecuniary misfortune that royal visitations often occasioned. Extreme measures, but clearly preferable to the Fleet Prison. More recent acclaim occurred when Hoghton Tower assumed the guise of a monastery in the very first episode of Cracker.

The Walk

No psychoanalysis needed on this walk, so return to the A6061 turning right for a walk back towards Riley Green. Bear left at the Royal Oak along the old driveway which swings away to the right up a hedged corridor after Green Lane Farm.

After mounting the ladder stile, fork away left to cross the field over another before reaching a small wood stiled at either side on

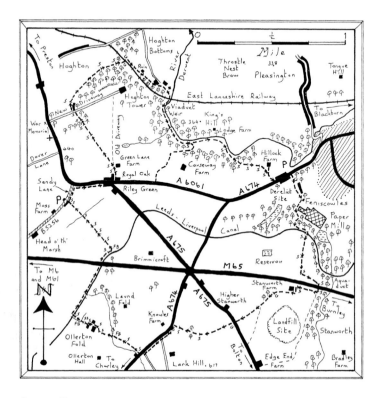

the small connecting passage. Then amble down to cross the new driveway serving Hoghton Towers adjacent to a lodge.

Accompany the enclosing wall all the way round the rising ground on your right over three stiles to enter the woodland on the north side of the hill. Go down to cross the railway, gated at each side, bearing hard right along its edge until a fenced passage angles you down past a pair of ruined cottages. Soon after the track brings you to the old mill settlement of Hoghton Bottoms.

Now converted to residences, the spinning and weaving of cotton finally ceased back in 1971, being one more casualty of cheap imports. Head right along the deep cutting of the River Derwent

From Hoghton Bottoms, accompany the Derwent upstream.

under the surging viaduct. Stick to this right side of the river upstream for a mile as it swings in a series of wide loops.

After the second stile the path forks uphill away from the river, emerging into a field above by a stile. Cut across half left for 100 metres to enter the next field by a stile, thereafter chaperoning the fence on the right along towards Hillock Farm. Mount a stile and cross the field half left to join the access track serving the farm down to the main road at Feniscowles.

Bear left for 200 metres, then immediately beyond some old houses on the opposite side, go through a gate and across derelict land once occupied by a paper mill. Stroll up towards the new mill and bear right at a gatehouse. The way, sandwiched between the mill and a wall, climbs up through some trees to join the Leeds-Liverpool Canal.

Bear left for 50 metres to cross the canal bridge and a stile heading due south up a rising grass shoulder. Mount a fence stile after 200 metres then aim for the left corner of a walled section. From here, slant down to go under the motorway bridge spanning the tree-lined River Roddlesworth. Climb up the far side to a stile adjacent to Stanworth Farm.

Head left then right to follow the access track down to the A675. Go straight over through a gate wandering alongside a hedge/wall. At the end of this long field, mount a fence stile then pass through a line of trees and another stile to reach the A674.

Head left along this main road for a quarter mile until a stile on the right points the way to Ollerton Fold. Beyond the first stile and after a footbridge on the left, cross to a wall stile. The right-of-way goes through a well-kept private garden so please respect the owner's diligence.

Drop down the far side to negotiate a route through this tiny hamlet. At the far side, a series of stiles will find you approaching the canal down a narrow corridor. Head right along the towpath until a stile 100 metres beyond the motorway bridge is located in the hedge. Cross a small footbridge and keeping the fence on your left, take a north westerly course mounting five more stiles to arrive back at Sandy Lane.

Taste the mystery of round loaf

An atmosphere of obscurity and imagination hovers atop the lonely Anglezarke Moor

Distance: 6 miles
Height: 600 feet (183 meters)

Summit Visited: Round Loaf 990 feet (302 metres)

Start/finish: At the northern end of Anglezarke Reservoir there are various pull-ins off the valley road

Terrain: A series of tapering reservoirs lie at the foot of extensive uplands with few landmarks

Explorer 19 *West Pennine Moors*

Shops etc.: Chorley

Prelude

Stretching away to the eastern horizon, Anglezarke Moor presents a bleak and lonely prospect – an ideal trek for walkers who enjoy their own company. Few of the visitors who flock to the country park in the valley below venture beyond the old workings of Lead Mines Clough. Nothing has changed here since time immemorial. A perfect place to commune with nature atop the remote hillock known as Round Loaf. But save it for a sunny afternoon. This is no place to be caught out when a dense mantle of clinging mist envelops the moor.

And don't be surprised if unexplained forces from the distant past make their presence felt, for Round Loaf is a man-made burial site from way back. Its heritage is steeped in mystery. Why ancient man should have chosen such an outlandish place to inter his dead has never been determined. But such places have exerted a powerful influence over local people for centuries.

Pagan ceremonies were performed here by Druid priests well before the dawn of Christianity and the 'tumulus' is thought to possess magical properties. Certainly Round Loaf is the most important Bronze Age site in Lancashire, being a focus for Ley Line activity. These are ancient links between primeval artefacts, their suggested purpose being for route finding.

Mystical connotations associated with witchcraft are still a facet of this remarkable mound, so a visit should not be undertaken lightly. With all this primitive energy permeating the atmosphere, a fine clear day will hopefully prevent you getting lost. No guidebook writer would want his readers being condemned for eternity to wander aimlessly across this desolate moor.

The Walk

Go through the kissing gate close to the northern end of Anglezarke following the east side of the controlled flow of the Goit upstream. After two hundred metres close to a footbridge the clear path leans away to the right but still parallels the river for a mile. Eventually, it arrives at an aqueduct and footpath coming in from White Coppice Farm. After crossing a footbridge the trail become cobbled, indicating that this was at one time a major link with Brinscall and its cotton mills.

Soon after crossing Dean Black Brook, watch for an abrupt bifurcation to the right which climbs steadily up the lower bracken-clad slopes to reach the ruin of White Stile House. Now barely more than a heap of stones, pass through the adjacent wall gap and continue heading due east over rough ground passing through numerous wall gaps.

Beyond a footbridge, the path leans to the left soon merging with another, skirting the southern flank of Brown Hill. After two hundred metres, pass a small coppice on the right to arrive at Drinkwater's. This untidy cluster of stones represented an abandoned farmstead with its own preserved well known as 'Joe's Cup'.

From here, leave the main path taking a thin trod through the grass over to the tree-lined depression occupied by Dean Black Brook.

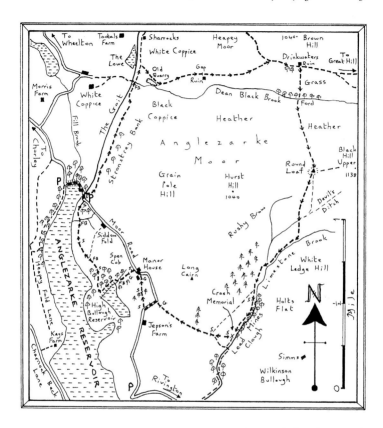

Ford the shallow waters to accompany a clear path heading south across a gently rising swathe of heather. Round Loaf only appears at the last minute, an oasis of lighter green resting on the level plateau like some alien spacecraft.

Surmounted by a small cairn, this is indeed a bewitching spot to imbibe the ambience of over three millennia. Ignore the unwelcome intrusion blighting the landscape on Winter Hill if you can. A variety of thin trails fork away from the hallowed ground like the spokes of a wheel.

The well known as 'Joe's Cup' supplied Drinkwaters.

The best option is to strike off across the stubbly moor in a slightly west of south direction taking the more prominent track. This will eventually bring you into the upper reaches of Limestone Brook, a shallow depression at this point hemmed in by tough moorland sedges. Head off downstream on a thin path. This becomes more pronounced as the deep cutting of the brook surrounded by dense tree cover is neared.

At the edge of the tree cover, fork left off this clear track through a stile after which the thin path is squeezed by a fence on the right.

Accompany the upper edge of Lead Mines Clough which is cloaked in thick bracken and lined with trees. The way is clear all the way down, finally emerging from the trees to reveal an open prospect beside a stone memorial.

Erected in 1955 by the Rotary Club of Horwich, it commemorates the crash of a Wellington bomber with the loss of six crew members on 12 November 1943.

Memorial to an aircraft that crashed on Anglezarke Moor.

> *In the valley below, substantial quantities of lead were once mined. But today Lead Mines Clough is a favourite picnic spot.*

Bear right from the memorial over a ladder stile then contour round the edge of the fell. After straddling another stile, the path soon merges with a clearer track that takes you all the way to Moor Road where you pass through Jepson's Gate.

Head left downhill for two hundred metres taking notice of the line of linked reservoirs stretching away to the south. Watch for a stile on the right after which the adjoining steeply canting field is crossed. Mount a stile located in a gap between a line of conifers thereafter keeping right of farm buildings. The road beside Manor House is gained through a gate, two adjacent stiles, then along a fenced passage to the exit.

Opposite the house, slant left through a stile followed soon after by another to descend steeply to valley level amidst overhanging trees. Beside High Bollough Reservoir on your left, cross a footbridge swinging hard left through the tree canopy. Keep right when the footpath divides at the edge of the trees. Another footbridge is crossed soon after a fence stile as we accompany the east side of Anglezarke Reservoir. The path is set back and above the waters providing a clear course all the way back to its northern limit where Moor Road is rejoined through a stile.

Head left back to the car and the culmination of a fine moorland trek over an ancient and mystical landscape. This is not the sort of walk in which to engage when a dank cloak of grey stuff hangs low over the moor. It would be easy to become lost, wandering forever in company with the spirits of our primeval forebears.

Make your way along the Ribble

A level playing field protected from riverine flooding by embankments

Distance: 6.5 miles
Height: Insignificant

Start/finish: Park in the village of Hutton along one of the side roads that branch off the old road now by-passed by the A59 dual carriageway. I chose Tolsey Drive between the roundabout and Hutton Grammar School

Terrain: Flat agricultural land slopes gradually down to the River Ribble

Explorer 286 *Preston and Blackburn*

Shops etc.: Hutton

Prelude

You will be hard pressed to find any mention of Hutton in the history books for Lancashire should the need arise to investigate this rather innocuous settlement. Little more than a collection of dispersed farms scattered across the flat plain south of the Ribble estuary, it has grown up in recent years as a commuter village. Two residential estates straddle the old winding road that has now been by-passed.

And Hutton could quite easily slip back into anonymity were it not for the presence of a celebrated and highly respected private grammar school. Another claim to prominence lies on the opposite side of the main road where the headquarters of Lancashire constabulary are housed. Watch out for the mounted division exercising their horses along the lanes hereabouts.

Hutton Women's Institute attained a degree of notoriety in the early

There has been a school on this site at Hulton since 1517.

years of the twentieth century in having the area's first suffragette as its secretary. This particular lady attempted to further the 'cause' by burning down the Rivington bungalow of Lord Leverhulme in 1913.

The Walk

Our walk begins by taking the stiled footpath opposite the grammar school heading north west along the right side of an intermittent line of trees. At the end of the field, ignore the stile that takes you into the adjoining field and continue with a hedge on your right. Pass between a house and small wood to reach Ratten Lane.

Offset to the left at the far side, the right-of-way continues over a stile along a constricted passage between houses. The path bends round to the right entering the field behind over another stile. Follow the right side of the long narrow pasture up to a fence stile just beyond Knowles Plantation. Keep ahead, accompanying the hedge on your right until it slopes down to a shallow valley occupied by Mill Brook.

Bear away from the hedge to mount a stile in the hedge, veering sharp left to follow this lethargic rill downstream. After 20 metres straddle a fence stile soon after bending right to a stile at the end. The way now heads due north along a raised tree-lined banking with the narrow stream on the right.

Beyond the next stile, carry on for a further half mile to reach the

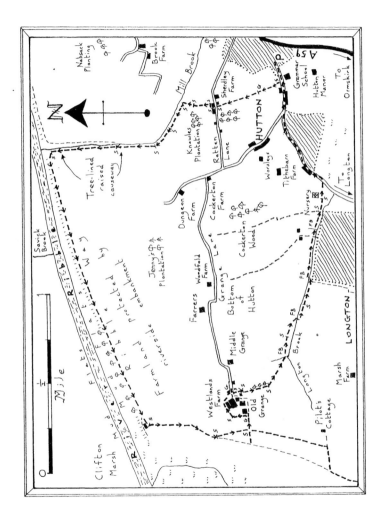

banks of the River Ribble. Across the far side can be seen traffic moving along the A583 between Preston and Lytham St Annes. A mile as the crow flies but a substantial detour by road or footpath, the nearest crossing point being Penwortham Bridge.

Once on the broad embankment that effectively prevents flooding of the low lying agriculture land behind, head left downstream towards the estuary. Keep to the lip of the abrupt banking. Below are the mud flats sloping down to the river itself. At high water mark an ugly line of tidal flotsam, mainly comprising the bleached bones of dead trees, mars the otherwise rustic idyll.

Almost two miles of walking along this section of the long distance route called the *Ribble Way* will bring you to an old brick water

Debris left by the rising tidal flow of the Ribble near its estuary.

treatment site. Continue ahead at your peril as Hutton Marsh is used by the wildfowlers of the area. Swing left away from the river over a fence stile and along the fenced embankment heading south.

After a half mile, watch for a sign and stile on the left that indicates a deviation from the original course of the Ribble Way. Cross the field using a slightly raised grass causeway. At the end, mount a stile and bear left along a track serving Westlands Farm. Do not enter the grounds but veer left through a gate to stroll alongside the fence on your right. After 200 metres, mount a stile on the right into the adjacent field to pass behind the farm building bearing to the right.

Aim for a gate at the far side to enter the start of Grange Lane. Bear right back towards the farm then take the stile on the left after 100 metres, followed soon after by another. Head across the fields beside a loose line of trees. Over a stile at the end, bear half left over to the far corner to cross a footbridge. Amble across the field to the next stile then lean in to a footbridge at the far right corner. Now on the far side of Longton Brook, walk alongside to the start of new housing on the edge of Longton.

We are now at the northern limit of Longton which has burgeoned into a commuter settlement for those working in the nearby towns. This has been due primarily to the flood-control measures implemented in the South Ribble area. Dating back to Anglo-Saxon times, the area was then almost inaccessible because of bogs, marshes and frequent inundation by the river.

It was a poor locality in the early nineteenth century with its own workhouse. The growth of the industrial towns allowed it to prosper later in the century when mill owners chose to live out here. Being a stopping point on the now dismantled coastal railway further stimulated growth. Hutton and Longton both grew up along the main Preston-Liverpool highway and have almost merged into a single built-up area.

The path crosses back over the brook on a footbridge and follows it along the backs of the houses all the way to the Hutton Road. Take a left back to your starting point.

Star billing for a curate

Astronomy and lawless exploits go hand in hand along the old road to Liverpool

Distance: 4 miles
Height: Insignificant

Start/finish: Park on one of the cut-off portions of the old Liverpool Road at the Southern edge of Much Hoole near to Lane House Farm

Terrain: Flat mainly arable farmland comprising large crop fields plus grazing land enclosed by hedges and fencing

Explorer 286 *Preston and Blackburn*

Shops etc.: Much Hoole

Prelude

Straggling the course of the old road between Preston and Liverpool, numerous villages hark back to a genteel age when vehicles moved at an infinitely more sedate pace. Twists and turns were no hindrance to the horse-drawn wagons of yesteryear, but are a nightmare for the impatient modern traveller. The new A59 cuts arrow straight across the flat plain avoiding most of the settlement and resultant bottlenecks.

Flat as a snooker table maybe, but this is ideal terrain for those who prefer their walking on the level. Its remote location amidst rural surroundings also ensures a degree of seclusion that I for one find preferable to the 'nodding donkey' syndrome encountered on more popular routes.

Primarily associated with farming traditions, Much Hoole is known to have helped in the shipping of Wigan coal to Ireland by way of the River Douglas. Flood control measures have helped turn waterlogged marshes into highly productive arable land and the embankment lining the river now prevents unwanted inundation at high tide.

Far more interesting, however, are the village's smuggling activities *when gin and lace were surreptitiously procured from Holland. Before the area was drained, travellers crossed the swampy lowlands at their peril. Known as 'Christ's Croft', it became a no-man's-land where brigands and footpads roamed at will. A lawless tract peopled by nebulous Will o' the Wisps. This short verse ably sums up the feelings of the age before enlightenment:*

> *When all England is aloft*
> *Safe are those that are in Christe's Croft*
> *And where should Christe's Croft be*
> *But between the Ribble and Mersey?*

Perhaps this association with illicit dealings is what persuaded the official hangman, Albert Pierrepoint, to become landlord of the Rose and Crown back in the 1950s.

The Walk

From the old road, walk south west to join the new highway. After only 100 metres a signpost on the right points the way across the fields. Keep a tree-lined brook on your left passing through two hedge gaps at the edge of the fields for a distance of a quarter mile. You will then be able to cross to the far side of the brook by means of a plank footbridge.

Continue heading in a general westerly direction towards the River Douglas which is hidden from view by the tall hedges. Soon, the path enters a hedged corridor that bends round to the left arriving at the top end of Haunders Lane close to Much Hoole House. Bear right over a stile and across the course of the old railway following a grass embankment over to the riverside.

Here the river provides sheltered accommodation for a large number of yachts on the opposite shore. When I passed this way, many of these had been hauled up onto dry land for maintenance work. All of them rely on engine power to negotiate the narrow channel that links with the Ribble estuary four miles to the north.

Heading left past the yacht basin, the path sticks to the elevated bank that prevents flooding of the rich farmland behind. After passing the

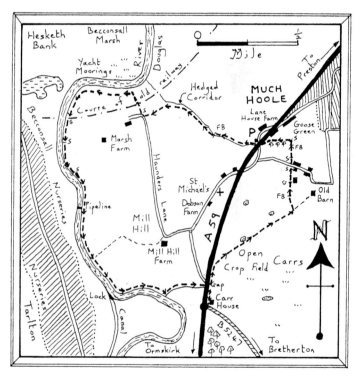

third stile, a pipeline is reached which spans the river. On the far side are the extensive nursery glasshouses of Becconsall and Tarleton. A half-mile further and the river swings left in a wide loop. Our route leaves the river at this point to slant left alongside a short tributary up to the main road.

Head right for 150 metres to a roundabout and then left along the B5247 to visit Carr House.

> *Hidden from casual view, this fine Stuart residence was built in 1613 by the Stone Brothers for a third brother who was engaged locally in raising sheep. Thomas and Andrew had made their fortune in haberdashery and wool which they exported to Europe.*

An unsung Lancashire hero, Jeremiah Horrocks, lived at Carr House.

The house is unusual in having an extended porch at the front and cage newel around which the staircase was built. It is a unique residence and one of only a couple in the whole of England. The front elevation is composed of red brick interlaced with an attractive cross-hatched pattern in blue. But its real claim to fame occurred in 1639 when the curate from St Michael's Church rented the room above the doorway.

From here, Jeremiah Horrocks made astronomical history by observing the transit of Venus across the face of the sun. Using primitive equipment, he plotted the movement on paper. No mean feat for a young man of only 21 years. His discovery led directly to Captain Cook's epic voyage to the South Seas where the renowned sailor was able to observe the transit of Venus from the shores of Tahiti in 1769.

This unsung Lancashire hero paved the way for modern space exploration and a crater on the Moon has been named after him. A plaque in the church announces that the event took place at 3.15 p.m. on Sunday, 24 November 1639. It is unfortunate that Jeremiah died two years later unable to fully capitalise on his genius. Perhaps if he had lived to a greater age, his renown would have been far more widespread. As it is, Carr House and its celebrated heritage has so far escaped the dubious attention of tourist exploitation.

Retrace your steps heading back towards Much Hoole. After crossing Carr House Bridge, watch for a stile in the hedge on the right which can be straddled. A clear path cuts across the large open field which was given over to oil seed rape on my visit.

About 200 metres before reaching a large old barn, cut left towards a fence where a footbridge is crossed. This will find you entering a grass

A plaque extolling the achievements of Jeremiah Horrocks can be viewed in St Michael's Church.

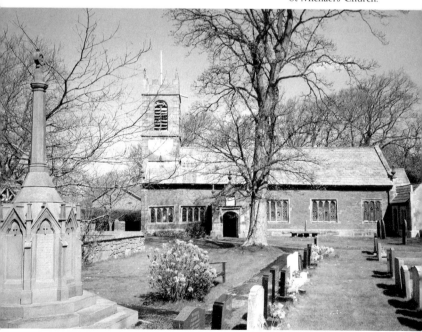

paddock. Head due north to pass through a fenced gate keeping left of the farm buildings to locate a stile hidden in the far right corner of the next field.

You will now be on a back lane at the eastern end of which is the old Manor House. Cross over this strip of tarmac to continue slightly offset to the left. The path mounts another stile followed by a footbridge after 100 metres to reach a stile at the far side close to some glasshouses.

Bear left under a tree-lined canopy keeping left of a fenced enclosure to gain the main road opposite the outward path. You are now heartily recommended to visit St Michael's Church.

Built in 1628 and made of Dutch brick, it boasts a magnificent walled sundial on the square bell tower. This was erected in 1875 with the motto Sine Sole Sileo *translated as 'Without the Sun I am silent'.*

Don't bottle out in Parbold

A circuit around one of South Lancashire's most prestigious hill top monuments

Distance: 5.5 miles
Height: 425 feet (130 metres)

Start/finish: Turn off the A5209 into Parbold Village. Immediately over the canal bridge, swing left into the car park

Terrain: Fenced off grass pasture of the sandstone foothills interrupted by large quarries and wooded glades

Explorer 285 *Southport and Chorley*

Shops etc.: Parbold

Prelude

Nudging out of the West Lancashire Plain, clusters of sandstone hills flex their muscles vying for our attention. Mere pimples when compared to their more lofty cousins to the east, they remain kings over all they survey in this primarily flat terrain. Such a pretender is Parbold Hill. Although only 300 feet high, it affords splendid views encompassing the whole area.

Surmounted by what appears to be a bottle of vintage port, this turns out to be a stone monument commemorating the Great Reform Act of 1832. In aloof isolation from a walker's point of view, it is best visited at the end of this fine ramble in conjunction with some refreshment at The Wiggin Tree.

Parbold Village lies at the bottom of the hill overlooked by the unmistakable 'Bottle'. Now almost completely submerged beneath a welter of commuter estates, the old heart is easily missed. The

The Parbold Bottle recalls the passing of the 1832 Great Reform Act.

settlement first grew up around farming, its most prominent feature being the mill. Now minus sails and grinding machinery, it stands at the core of the old village adjacent to the miller's house and the Windmill Inn.

The Leeds and Liverpool Canal used to carry local stone for construction in the expanding towns of Lancashire, and coal was sent to fire up the gasworks of Liverpool. Barges still line the canal bank but are now for leisure use only. It is easy to understand why many of the Lancashire cotton mill owners chose to settle in Parbold. Who can blame them: it certainly is a delectable village.

The Walk

From the car park, cross the bridge and accompany the canal towpath in a westerly direction passing beneath two bridges. Leave the towpath at Chapel House Farm erected on the site of the old Douglas Chapel built in 1526. Demolished in 1875, a cross to mark its passing was fashioned from the original stone in 1906.

Stroll across the canal bridge and up the lane for 150 metres to

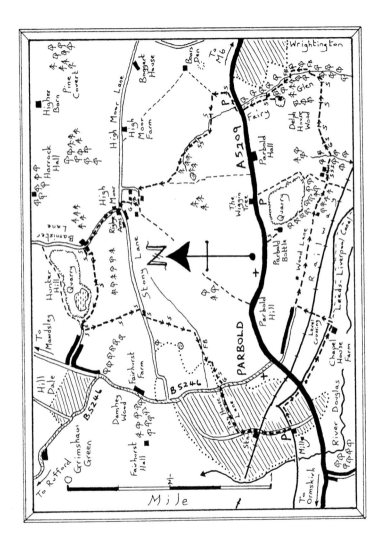

negotiate the level crossing. A similar distance ahead will bring you to a T-junction. Head right along Wood Lane that soon becomes a gravel track skirting the base of Parbold Hill. Trees on the left conceal a large stone quarry. Beyond Whitley Cottage, the path enters the tree cover.

At a walker's crossroads, go straight over past two houses where the right-of-way is channelled along a fenced section comprising three stiles. It then drops into a wooded glen and up the far side. Open a gate and then mount a stile to stroll along a fenced passage at the end of which is a stile giving onto a field. Accompany the fence on your right to the end of the field maintaining a direct course across the next one to enter the secluded vale of Sprodle Brook by a stile.

Slant immediately left to cross a footbridge and up some steps. The trail ascends this most charming of locales. At the well-named Fairy Glen, one can readily picture the little people skipping and cavorting up the turbulent falls in ecstatic glee. The clear path winds upward, re-crossing by another footbridge higher up before forking left up a flight of steps to join a quarry access road.

On reaching the main road, bear right for 200 metres to a parking zone on the opposite side where a stile is crossed into the adjacent field. Walk alongside a fence up to the corner then swing left along a wall to re-enter the upper wooded fringe of Sprodle Brook. Follow the path that squeezes into a fenced passage as far as a planting of conifers.

Stroll along the northern edge of the woods before striding over the infant brook and across open ground to fork into a field track. Head north to the outskirts of High Moor bearing left at a metalled lane, then right after 100 metres along a pinched corridor to reach High Moor Lane. Head left for 100 metres forking right past the Rigbye Arms for a quarter mile.

On reaching a renovated barn mount three stiles into the field behind. Amble along the back fence locating a thin trod heading west along an intermittent line of trees. After mounting a fence stile the path skirts the edge of a large disused quarry, beautiful in springtime, with a reedy tarn surrounded by clumps of yellow gorse.

The old windmill and its namesake pub beside the Leeds and Liverpool Canal.

At the bottom, join the quarry access lane soon mounting a stile on the left to follow a wall heading south along to its corner. Continue to the far side and another fence stile. Walk up beside the fence on your left to reach Stony Lane. Take a right down here leaving it after 50 metres only to mount a stile on the left side.

Make a half right crossing of this field to reach a fence stile offset to the left away from the path. Then aim for a tree-lined brook to cross a stream by means of a footbridge. Stick to the right hand side of the field walking behind houses on this outer edge of Parbold. A quarter mile down you will arrive at a stile and fenced passage adjoining a school. Cross straight over the B5246 and walk down Tan House Lane taking a left along the main street back the canal car park.

A beacon from the past

Stand alongside a past technology where fire was more than just a source of heat

Distance: 4 miles
Height: 350 feet (107 metres)

Start/finish: At the crossroads forming the hamlet of Dalton on the north east fringe of Skelmersdale, park on Elmers Green Lane opposite the St Michael and All Angels Church

Terrain: Rolling foothills of this rich farming landscape are interspersed with woodland and secluded glens

Explorer 285 *Southport and Chorley*

Shops etc.: Ashurst, a suburb of Skelmersdale

Prelude

Lying between the valleys of the Rivers Tawd and Douglas, a wedge of sandstone upland provides fine walking with very little effort. Interest is maintained throughout with an ever-changing pageantry of superb views to stimulate the optics. Coupled with an historical tradition stretching back through the centuries, this ramble is ideal for a clear afternoon when the grey stuff has gone walkabout elsewhere.

Dalton lies on the very edge of the sprawling township of Skelmersdale at the foot of this unique tract. It grew up on what must have been an important route focus at one time with its large church and school. Both are clustered around the site of an ancient hall where Sir William Ashurst once resided. It was he that erected the beacon which is the main focus of this walk.

The Walk

Walk down the lane past the church and take the first right along a track beside Ashurst Hall.

175

Ashurst Hall reputedly dates back to the fourteenth century.

All that remains of the original structure, said in 1640 to have been a 'large castellated edifice', is the stone doorway that is thought to be of fourteenth-century origin. Directly opposite is the 'Columbarium' which was restored to its former glory in 1985.

Go through a gate beside the dovecote overlooking a pond used by local anglers and make your way along a fenced path to a stile at the end. Cross over a field track into a hedged passage that takes you up to the edge of the woods surrounding Ashurst Hill. Bear right after the gate before striking up a steep section to gain the open prospect surmounted by the Ashurst Beacon.

This conspicuous monument with its pyramidal roof was erected in 1798 by Lord Skelmersdale when invasion by the forces of Napoleon was thought to be imminent. Soldiers were stationed here to light the beacon should the need arise. In the event it never was.

176

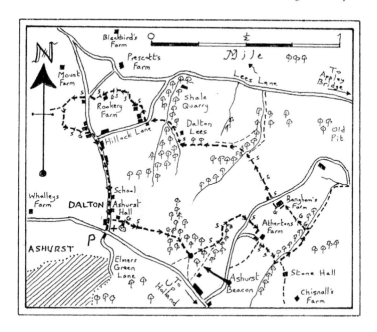

But the monument remains a prominent reminder of how communication was achieved at the opposite end of the spectrum from today's internet revolution. The beacon was presented to Wigan Corporation in 1962 as a civic amenity and is now a renowned beauty spot.

To its left is the Dalton Centenary Memorial erected in 1994 with a viewpoint indicator that shows Ormskirk Parish Church 5.5 miles distant as the crow flies. The farthest distance seen is the Isle of Man 84 miles away.

Continue past the memorial seat taking a north easterly course down into the woods to reach a wall corner. Mount the stile bearing right to follow the edge of the fenced wood down to a footbridge and stile at the bottom of the field. Accompany a hedged brook on the left bearing right along a fence at the end of this field to reach a back lane.

The Ashurst Beacon – a memorial to an invasion that never came in 1798.

Cross straight over to mount a stile and another soon after before slanting right up to the paved access road serving Atherton's Farm. Go into the yard and take a path hidden on the right to continue. Two more stiles will find you approaching a wood-fringed brook which is easily crossed. Climb out the far side to merge with the access track for Stone Hall.

Bear left down this for a quarter mile, keeping watch for the narrow path on the left that re-crosses the brook amid a sea of bluebells in Spring. Go through the gate and keep a fence on your left up to another gate on the approach to Bangham's Farm. Bear left around the edge of the farm buildings to join the access track which will bring you to the back lane crossed previously.

Take the wide field track opposite soon mounting a stile and accompany the hedge on your right to the end of the field. Maintaining this north westerly course, straddle two more stiles arriving at another wooded stream. Descend a zig-zag to cross the stream by a footbridge and stile bearing half left over to a fence on the far side of the large open field and a plank footbridge with stile. Do not cross to the far side. Instead, stroll along the fence to its end, then keep a straight course beside some trees until you reach another tree-lined brook. Bear right alongside the edge until a stile can be straddled. A clear track passes Dalton Lees eventually depositing you on Hillock Lane.

Bear left then almost immediately right along a clear track with some imposing residences to the left. The track swings to the left after 150 metres passing through a stile opposite Rookery Cottage (some cottage believe me). Follow the edge of the field round to follow yet another stream down to a stile. Once over this one, accompany the fence on your left through a stile and two gates to reach Rookery Farm.

Stroll through the farmyard and along the access track to arrive at a road junction. Cross over to mount the stile on the far side ambling along the hedge to the top of the field where the path leans half left. After 100 metres take a left to the edge of a fenced horse paddock. Cross to its far side passing through the gate and down a garden path. At the first outbuilding, bear right through a gate and follow a constricted passage between fencing to next door's driveway. A left will bring you out onto a road. Now head right for a half-mile stroll back to Dalton.

A martin's view of the mere

Wild and wonderful, the mossland of Martin Mere has achieved global acclamation

Distance: 5.5 miles
Height: Insignificant

Start/finish: Parking is restricted to a few roadside verges marked on the map. Alternatively, you could park at Martin Mere and start the walk from there if you decide to visit this most renowned of nature reserves. There again, you could take advantage of the railway that crosses the mosslands to start at New Lane Station. There is also space for one car adjacent to the electricity sub-station beside the railway at New Lane.

Terrain: Drained marshes characterise this part of the Lancashire Plain much of which is below sea level. Clear paths most of the way

Explorer 295 *Southport and Chorley*

Shops etc.: Burscough Bridge

Prelude

A suggestion was once made that a walk should be made available to those who depend on public transport. So here goes. This one came about when my normal means of conveyance broke down. A change of train at Wigan is involved. But there is no doubt that New Lane station makes the ideal starting point for a walk across the ancient lake bed of Martin Mere. If you do decide to go by train, it makes perfect sense to include a trip round the wildlife sanctuary. Your time there will not be wasted.

This flat expanse of West Lancashire offers some of the richest cropland in the country. In the seventeenth century, you would have been forced to walk 18 miles to make a complete circuit of these submerged tracts. Drainage was deemed necessary to grow food for the burgeoning populations of expanding Lancashire townships such as Liverpool and Wigan. Numerous failed attempts to drain the Mere resulted in the designer of the highly successful Bridgewater Canal, James Brindley, being engaged to solve the problem.

It was to be almost a century before the first crops were finally harvested. Today large open fields crammed with wheat, potatoes, carrots and leeks to name but a sample 'sprout' from the rich black soils. This is made possible by a dense network of dykes that feed into a large drainage canal emptying into the estuary of the River Ribble.

The Walk

Set off from New Lane Station by walking along the road on the north side for 300 metres until a path forks off right at a sharp bend. Make a beeline for the railway and follow it for 300 metres. This section is unused and in dire need of trampling. Do your best as others will hopefully follow.

On reaching a cross-track, bear left along this past a lone hawthorn and onward to the next pair of trees. Another 200 metres will see you bending right to pass on the north side of Monks Farm. The right-of-way at this point has been diverted slightly away from the farm buildings. Join the main access track bearing left up to the corner of a back lane.

Take another left up a clear field track across Marsh Moss for a half mile all the way to Brandreth Farm. A right swerve behind a pond is needed to reach Tarlscough Lane. Head left for a quarter mile and keep a sharp eye open for the narrow track that circumvents Martin Mere on the left. A high fence and electric wires surround the compound. One can only speculate as to whether this is to keep the birds inside or non-paying interlopers out.

At the corner, swing hard right across the back to its far end where a large hide looks out over the wildfowl reserve.

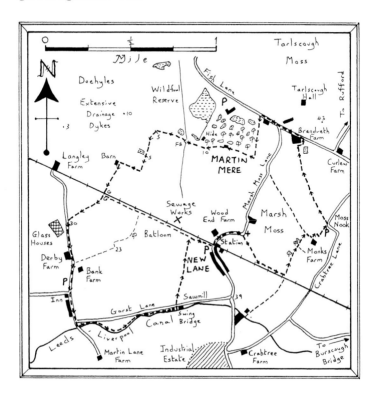

Ensconced within a fringe of trees, it is impossible to see anything from the outside. If it's the reserve that has attracted you to this walk, then it will be necessary to wander round to the front to gain admittance.

Covering 376 acres, it is one of numerous wetland sites under the control of the Wildfowl and Wetlands Trust which was founded by the late Sir Peter Scott in 1946. The centre is open all year except Christmas Day, and organises a wide range of events at regular intervals to suit all tastes.

In addition to providing a staging post for thousands of migrating wildfowl in autumn and winter, the site offers a permanent

An observation deck at the rear of Martin Mere Bird Sanctuary.

home to 1,500 tame birds from different parts of the world. By means of conservation programmes, education and research, the Trust is helping to save threatened species by managing the wetlands for future generations to enjoy. Winter refuge for over one hundred thousand ducks, geese and swans is offered at the WWT centres every year.

On the south-west edge of the site just beyond a large hide cross the main dyke by means of two footbridges. Then continue in a westerly direction for a further quarter mile. When the fence bends to the left mount a stile to head south. Straddle another stile adjacent to a newly excavated ditch. At the end of the next field boundary, swing right along to an isolated barn.

Stroll down the field track to cross the railway. If preferred, you can follow it back to New Lane at a brisk trot should the notion suddenly have occurred to you that today is your partner's birthday. Less forgetful walkers should continue down to join a back lane opposite some glasshouses. Bear left passing the appropriately named Martin Inn to reach a sharp left hander.

Keep ahead for a further 300 metres to join the canal. Take an easterly direction ambling along the towpath for a half mile. Leave this at a swing bridge to cross straight over Gorst Lane beside a sawmill. Accompany the track opposite back to the railway where a right will return you to New Lane Station.

The reserve on drained land attracts an international following.

The unknown face of Burscough

The past struggles manfully to maintain a precarious footing in the new millennium

Distance: 5 miles
Height: Insignificant

Start/finish: Turn off the A59 in Burscough opposite the Bull and Dog down Abbey Lane and park on the grass verge just beyond the exit from the council Waste Disposal site

Terrain: Rich open farmland, flat as a snooker table where rights-of-way follow the edges of the fields

Explorer 2: 85 *Southport and Chorley*

Shops etc.: Burscough

Prelude

Straddling the main road between Preston and Liverpool, the ancient settlement of Burscough lies on the edge of Martin Mere. On higher ground than the drained marshlands, it grew to importance as a transit junction, with two railway stations on lines that were at one time connected. Today both railways are independent of each other. The Leeds and Liverpool Canal also passes through Burscough carrying cruisers which view time as an irrelevance.

Originally a farming community with corn milling, basketry and cheese production predominating, it was the canal arriving here in 1775 that witnessed a huge growth in Burscough's population. This enabled several mills to flourish, the milled grain being distributed along the canal.

The town's central location meant that stables were established to house the horses that pulled the barges. They likewise required feed which was also prepared here for onward transit by the 'provender boat' for use on other canals.

Not many who pass through this elongated village will realise the importance it once held as a seat of monastic enterprise. Founded in 1124 by Robert de Latham and administered by the Black Canons of the Augustinian order, the priory flourished to such an extent that the monks were able to claim the rights and tolls from a weekly market held at nearby Ormskirk.

The influential Stanley family also recognised the priory's influence by electing to be interred within its vaults. Indeed it was Lord Stanley who retrieved the crown of Richard III at the Battle of Bosworth thus heralding the start of the Tudor dynasty.

Its days were finally numbered in 1536 when Henry VIII dissolved the monasteries. Stonework was removed but more significant was the

Burscough conceals the remains of Lancashire's forgotten priory.

relocation of the bells that once summoned the brethren to prayer. They were re-housed in Ormskirk Church in a custom-built steeple. This church is one of only three in England with both a spire and a tower.

The Walk

Continue down Abbey lane which terminates in the yard of a new industrial unit. Our route forks right along a hedged track which soon crosses the railway line. Another 100 metres brings us to Abbey Farm on the left. Alongside the wall on your left can be seen the remnants of the once proud edifice that has given the farm its illustrious name. Now on private land, only a few sections of walling and an archway remain of Lancashire's forgotten priory which is overshadowed by a large caravan park behind.

Keep straight ahead down the paved access road to reach Blythe Lane. Then bear left for 150 metres. Immediately after crossing Abbey Bridge, take a right turning to follow the edge of the field beside New Park Brook, here fenced off and lined with trees.

On reaching a field track, those of you with a pressing engagement at the tax office will need to take the short cut left towards Needless Inn Farm. Daring individuals who live life on the edge should carry on over the next field which is likely to be an ocean of heaving golden wheat if summer is your preferred season for visiting Burscough. You will then need to keep to the edge to avoid damaging the crop. Aim for a white gate, a mere 150 metres at the far side fronting a line of trees.

This needs to be climbed and is followed soon after by a fence stile giving access to private grounds through which the right-of-way traverses. Keep right of the tennis courts, walking along the edge of the trees to gain the access road serving the house. Then stroll down to a crossroads taking a left along Cranes Lane. Paved until just beyond the golf course entrance, it then heads due east, clearly a major thoroughfare in days gone by.

A thin stretch of woodland known as Mains Wood lies halfway along Cranes Lane and is accessible by a gap on the left. The hedged path

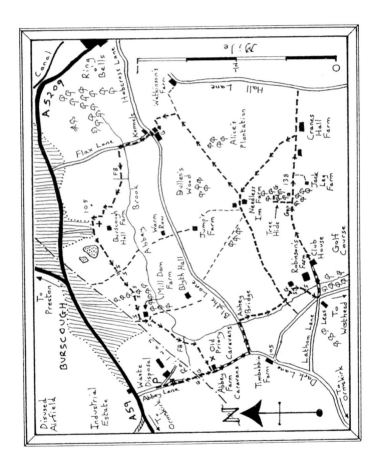

allows access to this preserve of the Woodland Trust. A short stroll for 200 metres followed by a right wheel will bring you into the confines of this preserved wildlife habitat.

It affords a natural haven where flora and fauna can flourish undisturbed by the ravages of agriculture progress. A tree hide in the centre is dominated by rhododendrons.

Returning to the main track, you will soon pass the entrance to kennels at Jack Leg Farm – surely nobody but a pirate turned landlubber could boast such a lyrical appendage.

After a further 300 metres, just beyond a row of houses, take a sharp left for the walk over to Needless Inn Farm chaperoned by a hedge on your left.

Was this abode once a hostelry serving the needs of thirsty travellers? A brief scan of the local Ordnance Survey map indicates the farm is a meeting point for numerous rights-of-way.

Bear right here along the edge of open fields past Bullens Wood to the left. On meeting a hedge, keep to its right side past Alice's Plantation on your right heading north east until opposite some houses on the left. Slant left here along the edge of another field up to its corner, then left again along the rear of the houses until a gate allows passage between the houses to reach Blythe Lane.

Bear right along here for 100 metres then left down Flax Lane at Qualco kennels. This building used to be a pub when the linen industry was in full swing hereabouts. Just after the road crosses Abbey Brook, head left along the edge of the field and over a footbridge at the far side.

(NB: On my last visit to this area, I was informed by a local dog-walker that the position followed by this 200 yard section of pathway along the edge of the field was in dispute. The landowner claims it should follow the top of the rough banking on your right. There certainly is a right-of-way along here. When you arrive its current course might well have changed.)

After crossing the footbridge, accompany the hedge on your right

Crops thrive on the rich black soil of the South Lancashire Plain.

until a clear grass track breaks right following a zigzag that emerges behind the chapel on the edge of a new housing development. Cross straight over the new road into a dark tunnel overhung by trees, mounting a stile at the end into the adjoining field. Make a half right slanting away from a fishing lake and aiming for the midpoint of a fence at the far side.

Cross a fenced field track stiled at each side and continue across the next field towards the line of trees ahead. Squeezed between stiled fencing, the path then makes for the access road serving Mill Dam Farm. Head left then right along a fence to enter the field at the far side. Keep to the right of Abbey Brook as it swing to the left.

After crossing a footbridge, follow the field boundary round to pass the remains of the old priory that can be seen in the well-tended garden behind the farm. On reaching Abbey Lane, retrace your steps back to the start having completed a fine ramble amidst the rich farmland of rural Lancashire.

ᴀ haunting at Heskin

Spirited intrigue invites you to unravel
the mystery surrounding yet another White Lady

Distance: 5.5 miles
Height: Insignificant

Start/finish: Various pull-ins are available on the road
from Anderton's Mill and at the junction by Barmskin Hall
with its wide grass verge

Terrain: Relatively flat, this higher ground comprising smaller fields than those in West Lancashire remains the
preserve of grazing animals rather than arable crops

Explorer 285 *Southport and Chorley*

Shops etc.: Eccleston near Charnock Richard

Prelude

*Away from the billiard table flatness that comprises much of West
Lancashire, a gently undulating landscape emerges the further east we
travel. Barely discernible, it might come as a surprise that this walk,
although incorporating very little uphill perambulation, touches the 65
metre contour. Around here there are far more smaller enclosed fields
where animal grazing takes precedence. Small towns lie dotted about
of which Eccleston is a prime example.*

*In days gone by, the locality at the start of this walk in South
Lancashire was renowned for the brewing of a particularly fine beer.
Barmskin refers to the coating that formed over the mash during the
process of fermentation. The nearest hostelry today is to be found a
quarter mile down the road to the south east along the aptly named
Toogood (to be true) Lane.*

The Walk

At the road junction a half-mile east of Anderton's Mill and near the entrance to Barmskin Hall Farm, mount a stile in the hedge. Aim half left to mount two others in quick succession before crossing a larger field to another at the far side of Howe Brook. Pass to the right of a tiny copse strolling alongside a fence to reach Town Lane. Bear left for 100 metres then mount the stile on the far side. With the hedge on your left, straddle another stile followed by a footbridge soon after arriving at a hedged field track.

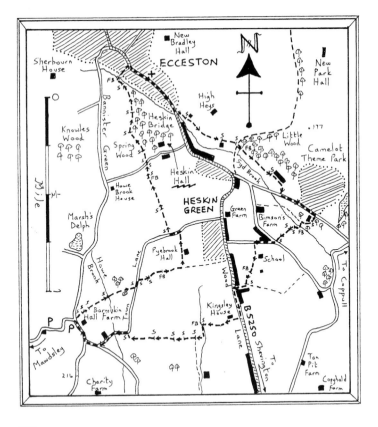

The White Lady is said to wander the corridors of Heskin Hall.

Accompany this initially round to the left past Pyebrook Hall then due north down the access track to rejoin Town Lane. Head left for 100 metres mounting a stile on the right. Head north alongside the hedge on your right leaping a stile and later passing through a small wood with footbridge and stile. You finally need to cross a small field to reach the access road serving Heskin Hall Farm.

Our route lies straight across, but first head right to take a look at Heskin Hall.

Although this building if of Elizabethan origin, it is often referred to as the 'new hall', the old one having long since fallen into decay. Today it is a management training centre and antiques warehouse. Many of the original residents were Roman Catholics. A ghostly apparition known as the White Lady of Heskin is reputed to walk the gloomy corridors of the hall. She was the landowner's 16-year-old daughter and was hanged by a Catholic priest who was captured whilst in hiding at the hall. A coward to the last, he attempted to deny his faith and thus save his own skin by stringing the poor girl to a beam in an attempt to prove he was an 'avid Protestant'. The beam can still be seen, and later visitors to the hall were often told to 'touch the hanging beam' for luck.

Another theory relates to the old chest at the foot of the grand staircase. The "White Lady" is said to be the spirit of a young girl who played a game on her husband by hiding in the chest. Unfortunately it fell shut and could not be opened. When her body was discovered some time later, the distraught man was inconsolable.

Continue the walk by following the western edge of Spring Wood all the way to the end where a stile allows entry to the tree cover. Keep ahead to cross Syd Brook by a footbridge then stroll up a passage to reach the main street of Eccleston opposite the Brown Cow. Bear right passing the Catholic Church of St Agnes built in 1922. Before that time, services had been held in a fish and chip shop on the site.

Continue down the main street until Heskin Bridge is reached then cross over taking the track to High Heys Farm. Bear right after 100 metres over a stile to follow the edge of a line of trees on the left. Approaching a solid fence, a hidden stile on the left edge allows entry to the adjacent field. Follow the top fence to gain a major track by a green tubular stile.

Bear right then left to cross a footbridge continuing along the edge of Little Wood on the left. A stile gives onto a rough lane with houses on one side. Rejoin Park Hall Road heading left for a quarter mile. Shrieks of laughter may be heard drifting over the high hedge on your left. They stem from the Camelot Theme Park.

Watch for a signpost on the right and a path through the trees. Mount a stile and swing right along a clear track that drops down in to open woodland then over to a footbridge spanning Syd Brook. Climb a set of steps heaving right over a stile to emerge into the field on the far side.

Aim for a stile in the hedge in front then stroll on to join Withington Lane at a Y-junction. Take the left arm past the Methodist church slanting left to pass the local primary school. Keep to the right of a lawn entering a narrow corridor at the end. This will lead you down to cross a small brook by a footbridge. Accompany the right bank of

St Agnes Church at Eccleston, built in 1922.

the tiny tributary mounting a gentle grass slope to reach a housing road. Bear right to reach Wood Lane. Then head left for 200 metres swinging right through the farmyard of Kingsley House. Maintain a straight course over the fields behind until a stile and footbridge are reached. Bear left then right after only 150 metres to the edge of the field, mounting a stile and another immediately after slightly offset to the right.

Thereafter maintain a westerly course for half a mile, mounting four more stiles to reach Town Lane. Head left then right at the first road junction followed by another right for the return to Barmskin.

Going up in the world

Ungodly influences struggle for ascendancy in this centre of spiritual accord

WALK 37

Distance: 5.5 miles
Height: 400 feet (122 metres)

Start/finish: Park on Brooklands Road near the old church of St Thomas the Martyr in the preserved heart of Upholland

Terrain: A rustic farming enclave sandwiched between urban developments and golf courses. The nature trail alongside Dean Brook is a joy to follow

Explorer 285 *Southport and Chorley*

Shops etc.: Upholland

Prelude

Only a small section of sandstone walling beside the Conservative Club remains of the old priory that once dominated life in Upholland. Built in 1307, the remainder has been incorporated into the adjacent church of St Thomas the Martyr. Its small tower dates from the fifteenth century; the original intention was for it to be much bigger. Unfortunately the money ran out resulting in the present diminutive, but no less impressive, structure.

Founded by Sir Robert de Holland, the fortunes of this proud knight were severely curtailed when he backed the wrong side against Edward II. His reward was to be exiled and reduced to begging on the streets of Flanders. A sad life was finally cut short on his return journey to England when his ship sank and he was drowned near Dover.

At the top end of the graveyard is to be found the 'robber's grave'. George Lyons was reckoned to be Lancashire's answer to Robin Hood and here he followed a similar gambit by robbing the rich to give to

Search out the robber's grave behind St Thomas the Martyr church in Upholland.

the poor. Unfortunately a lethal necktie awaited the legendary rogue after he was caught stealing bread from the nearby Owl Inn.

This whole area of old Upholland is now under a preservation order and is said to be awash with paranormal activity. Ellen Weeton's early nineteenth-century Journal of a Governess assures readers that ten per cent of the houses are haunted and 'scarcely a field or stile is without its attendant spirit'. Let me know if you spot any during the walk which begins along Brooklands Road.

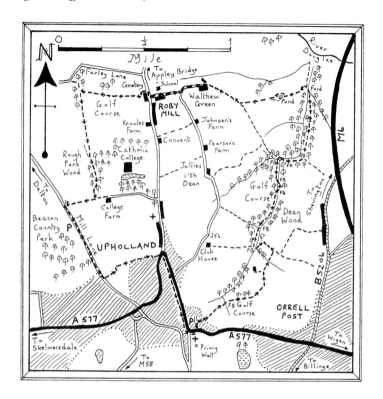

The Walk

Turn down Mill House View which branches right and at the end of which a thin path forges a route through dense undergrowth. It terminates at a footbridge that deposits you on the golf course. Keep left to accompany a line of trees across the mowed turf to the far side where a gate opens onto a stony track. Continue ahead along this, veering left after 200 metres.

When this broad track slants left to a barn, take the right hand arm that narrows before crossing a brook 100 metres further on. Bear left at the T-junction over to the tree-lined cutting occupied by Dean

Brook. The path swings left and down into the enclosed confines of the wood, surmounting two footbridges to gain the far bank.

Head downstream keeping to the lower path that follows the babbling brook as it meanders down to join the River Douglas. Although the next mile comprises a charming and delectable stroll, it is muddy in places even in dry weather due to the damp enclosed conditions in this girdled stretch. A pair of footbridges help in avoiding a steep section of banking and are followed by another two further along the valley.

After crossing the second of these, the path climbs away from the watercourse up its right bank. As the edge of the tree cover is neared, take a narrow side trail that branches left. Meandering through the trees, the thin trail descends gradually crossing an unusual log stile

The old farming hamlet of Walthew Green.

followed soon after by a conventional one.

When you reach Dean Brook, cross over to the opposite side forking left away from the stream up the far bank. Watch for a sharp branch to the left that will bring you out into an open field above. Head west along the left hand edge until a pond is reached surrounded by trees. Keep right of this as the path widens with a hedge on the left.

It soon merges with a major field track called Whitley Road that was clearly an important link route in times past. On arriving at the ancient farming hamlet of Walthew Green, the track becomes metalled up to Roby Mill and the road connecting Appley Bridge with Upholland. Bear right for 50 metres then swing left behind a cottage before continuing in a westerly direction with a hedge on your left and the cemetery to the right.

The right-of-way crosses a golf course and then makes a gradual ascent to reach the tree line at the far side. Head left here along the top side of a field in a southerly direction all the way to Rough Park Wood. On the left can be seen the rooftops of the Catholic College. Once used to train men for the priesthood, it is now a conference centre and retreat.

Our way kinks to the right at the edge of the woodland then follows a broad highway that has been cut through the trees. At the T-junction, bear right up to Mill Lane then left down here for a quarter mile until a signpost is reached just before a line of houses. It points the way to the left over the fields.

After a bend to the left, the path continues onward soon reaching the edge of a housing estate. Here it narrows considerably. At the end bear right then left down a ginnel to reach a road junction. Take the left arm back to the centre of Upholland and another search for that illusive grave of George Lyons.

Mischief at Mawdesley

*Poke into tales of hell-fire and damnation in the company
of the ubiquitous White Lady*

Distance: 4 miles
Height: Insignificant

Start/finish: On the road into Mawdesley from Eccleston,
turn off onto some rough ground near an old quarry.
This lies opposite the war memorial 100 metres past
the Black Bull Inn

Terrain: Paths that are not in regular use cross hedged
fields where farm animals graze

Explorer 285 *Southport and Chorley*

Shops etc.: Mawdesley

Prelude

*Just to the right of our parking spot, up a flight of steps carved from
the solid rock, lies Mawdesley Hall. Unseen from the road, this half-
timbered farming residence dates from 1625. Parts are built of the
red sandstone dug from the quarry on the opposite side of the road.
Watch out for the mysterious 'White Lady' who supposedly haunts
the Hall.*

*Up the road is the Black Bull Inn. Now a quiet country pub, it was
once a hangout for local ruffians, with fearsome brawls a regular feature of the Saturday night entertainment. As a result it became known
as 'Hell Hob'. Revellers would sit round a roaring fire and boast of
sitting on the 'Hob of Hell Fire'. A huge poker hanging by the side of
the hearth and weighing in at sixteen pounds was used to stoke up
Old Nick's mischief and bets were placed on who could wield it with
the greatest dexterity.*

*One landlord claimed to have imprisoned in a bottle the spirit of
an old woman who haunted nearby Mawdesley Hall. His aim was to*

attract more custom to his drinking den. But fearing that the potent influence of the incarcerated phantom might rebound onto him, the superstitious host threw the bottle into a nearby pit, where it resides to this day.

The Walk

Stroll down the track towards the quarry veering right over a stile, then follow the edge of the field round to a footbridge opening onto a new housing development. Walk along the road and at the top end, bear left adjacent to a children's playground crossing a metal strip footbridge. Now head south west alongside the hedge on your left.

Pass through three field gaps to arrive at a stile, followed soon after by another combined with a footbridge. With the hedge now on your right, stroll to the field end where a pinched corridor will bring you

Mawdesley Hall has its own ghost in residence.

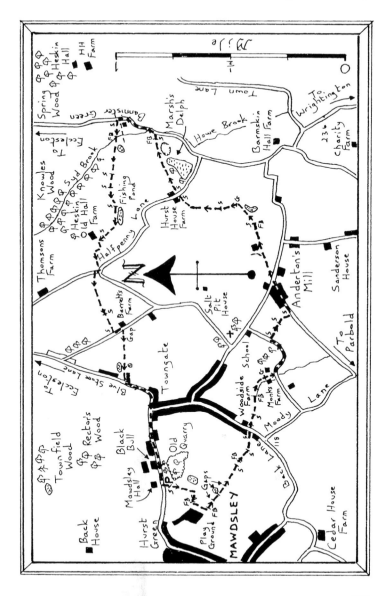

The Black Bull used to be known as 'Hell Hob'.

out onto Back Lane. Go straight across along the pathway to the right of Woodside Farm and down a fenced corridor to gain the back field over a stile.

Hemmed into a small brook by a fence, follow it all the way round to Monk's Farm. Enter the yard by a gate and exit down the driveway to bear left along a back lane. After a quarter mile take the path on the right over a stile. With the hedge on your right, stroll along the field edge to reach Bently Lane.

Head left into the old hamlet of Anderton's Mill. At a crossroads, keep ahead along a rough track. When it veers to the left, keep a straight line down a narrow passage beside a large garden. When I last came down here it had a single-track narrow gauge railway that appears to have gone out of use. Cross a footbridge followed soon after by a fence stile which will find you passing left of a fishing pond – one of many in this locality.

At the far side, straddle a difficult gate aiming half left to mount a stile in the facing hedge. Then make a beeline for Hurst House Farm at the far side of the field. Go through the farmyard to cross Halfpenny Lane. Mount a stile on the opposite side to cross a large field. Keep to the right where a quarry known as Marsh's Delph is hidden from view behind a screen of trees.

Fork in to join a fence strolling down to cross a footbridge and stile to reach Bannister Green. Head left along the road for 300 metres until a sign-posted right-of-way is reached on the left. Head west alongside a fenced track then fork away left after squeezing through a line of hawthorn trees. Aim to cross Howe Brook footbridge then strike out across the field keeping right of a pond.

Mount two hedge stiles in quick succession then stroll alongside the fence on your left to reach a fishing pond. Pass it on the left to accompany the fence bearing right around to another stile, keeping left of Heskin Old Hall Farm. Stick with the access track that will deposit you at a Y-junction.

On its far side enter a field to accompany a fence on the left straddling a stile after 200 metres. Continue onward to join Salt Pit Lane over a stile. Bear left for 100 metres until you see a narrow gap in the hedge opposite Barretts Farm. Stroll down the side of the field entering a narrow fenced passage that will bring you out onto Blue Stone Lane.

Bear left along here back into Mawdesley. Those who enjoy the macabre can be further stimulated by carrying on to Four Lane Ends in the village centre. Finch Cottage is named after the family who kept the preserved skull of a distant relative in a hidden chapel. These were the only remains of William Haydock, a Cistercian monk from Whalley Abbey, who was executed in 1536 for his contrary beliefs. Mary Haydock was the descendant who brought the relic to Mawdesley from Cottam Hall on The Fylde after marrying Thomas Finch. Mary's brother Cuthbert was also a priest and it was he who established the hidden chapel. Here it was that they created a shrine on account of the reputed healing properties of the skull.

Skulduggery at Appley Bridge

More concerning the persecution of Catholics in ye olde county of Lancashire

Distance: 5 miles

Height: 200 feet (61 metres)

Start/finish: A half mile before crossing the M6 when driving from Appley Bridge to Shevington, turn right and park on Broadriding Lane

Terrain: Reclaimed countryside from derelict coal mining sites fringed by wooded glens

Explorer 285 *Southport and Chorley*

Shops etc.: Appley Bridge near Skelmersdale

Prelude

Only a handful of dwellings have captured the imagination in Lancashire. Skull House is one of them. Hidden away on the northern fringe of Appley Bridge, this mysterious residence is easily missed. It has acquired a mystical reputation on account of the skull that has lived here for centuries and now rests proudly in a box in the living room.

Windows decorated with skulls commemorate a specimen whose origins are shrouded in mystery. The house itself is riddled with old passages and secret hides that were common at the time it was built in the first Elizabethan era. Mysterious cupboards and hideouts for priests were a common feature built into these old houses at a time when the faith of Catholics was being tested to the limit.

Some claim the skull was that of a knight in the age of King Arthur. I prefer the notion that it belonged to a priest on the run from

Skull House at Appley Bridge was a focus of religious fervour in centuries past.

Cromwell's troops during the Civil War. Hiding up the large chimney, a fire lit in the grate forced the unfortunate cleric to surrender whereupon he was promptly beheaded. The rest of his body is thought to be buried in the garden.

Whatever its pedigree, misfortune is said to befall the owners should the skull ever be removed. Once thrown into the River Douglas, it somehow arrived back at Skull House where it has been ever since. Though not strictly part of this walk, Skull House is well worth seeking out.

The Walk

Our walk begins on the far side of Appley Bridge walking along the road towards Shevington. At the end of the houses, take the footpath forking right over a stile and along the edge of some allotments. Bending left at the top end of the field, head due east for 150 metres to join the access track serving Broadridings Farm. You will soon fork right along a fenced passage through two kissing gates to cross Gathurst Golf Course.

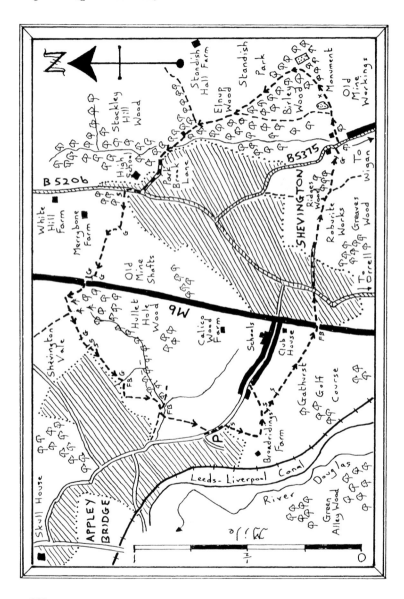

Watch out for flying balls as you pad cross the fairways making a beeline for the footbridge over the M6. At the far side, a fenced corridor allows passage through a housing estate in Shevington. Cross straight over the B5206 to continue along a residential road to the outskirts where it narrows into the service road for the Roburite Explosives Works.

> *This is an appropriate site as Shevington's prosperity has been founded on coal since 1350. Indeed no fewer than 53 pit shafts were discovered when the M6 was under construction. Today all the pits have closed and there is little on the surface to indicate the passing of a once vital resource. Small town or large village, Shevington has become a predominantly commuter settlement with easy access to the motorway, its population swelling twelve-fold over the last century.*

The right-of-way becomes a track beyond the works. Watch for a left fork when the main track veers to the right. Stroll down a shallow gradient alongside a fence going through a gate before eventually reaching the B5375. Bear right for 50 metres then take the track that continues on the far side across open land interspersed with trees and fishing ponds. This is an area that stands upon the subterranean arteries of old mine workings. Much of the land had now been reclaimed for leisure usage.

Take note of a small stone monument with pitched roof on the left maintained by the 'Friends of War Memorials'. Clearly it is dedicated to local miners who gave their lives in the service of their country. Stick with a clear path through the trees until a reservoir is reached. At this point, the path swings to the left. Avoid all red herrings that lead you back into the heart of Birley Wood. Keep heading generally east to gain the edge of the woodland beyond which stretches the open pasture of Standish Park.

A clear path can then be followed alongside a fence heading north. After almost a mile, it veers in towards the enclosed cutting chiselled out by Mill Brook. Now much wider, the path leans in to parallel the backs of housing and soon becomes the paved highway known as Park Brook Lane.

A memorial to coal miners who died for their country.

Keep to this residential road past the High School to merge with the B5206 heading right for 150 metres until a path can be taken on the far side. Go through the kissing gate and follow a narrow hedged track that will find you approaching the motorway. Pass through two gates and along a passage to cross over using a footbridge.

Once in the trees at the far side, bear half right to the edge of the tree cover, then left to reach a field track. Bear right for 50 metres then hard left to cross an open field in a straight line to the far side. Go through a gate followed by two stiles to amble along the backs of a housing estate called Shevington Vale.

At the bottom edge of this field, lean into the gully through a gate to pass, but not cross, a footbridge. Continue along the tree line, bearing left down to merge with another track at the far side that parallels another tree-lined brook. bear right to cross a track and then the brook via a footbridge. A gentle climb will return you to the Appley Bridge road alongside an intermittent hedge.

Crank it up at Billinge

Too much rabbiting on is not good for the health

Distance: 4 miles
Height: 450 feet (137 metres)

Start/finish: Parking is limited to a narrow pull-in
on the west side of Billinge Hill 200m up from the entrance to
Houghwood Golf Club

Terrain: A surging upthrust of sandstone, Billinge Hill
is one of a number that slope down to merge with the flat
expanse of the Lancashire Plain

Explorer 285 *Southport and Chorley*

Shops etc.: Billinge

Prelude

Look carefully around whilst walking up Crank Road towards Shaley
Brow. Beneath the overhanging canopy of trees that chaperone the
climb lurks the ghost of a white rabbit. For it was along this lonely
stretch that a nasty incident occurred some time in the distant past.

A rather unsavoury farmer named 'Old Nick' had taken it into his
head that an old woman living nearby was an emissary of the devil
trying to bewitch him. Along with an accomplice called Dick Piers, he
crept into her cottage with homicidal intentions. Woken by the disturb-
ance, the old woman and her young granddaughter fled the scene.
Unfortunately, young Jenny had to leave her pet rabbit behind.

So incensed was Dick Piers at having been thwarted that he kicked
the poor creature to death. The young girl also failed to make it
through the night. Exhaustion and fear caused a fall and she broke her
neck. Thinking he had escaped retribution for such a brutal assault,
Piers celebrated in this usual manner only to be confronted by the
rabbit on his way home.

In stark terror, he raced off to escape the frightful apparition. Next *day, his battered corpse was discovered in the quarry below Billinge Beacon. So if you do chance upon a rabbit during this ramble, treat it kindly.*

The Walk

Watch for a gap in the trees about 50 metres up the hill on the left. A narrow path will bring you out into a field via a fence stile. Accompany the fence on your left to the end of the field bearing right up the easy slopes before mounting a stile into the next field. Keep to its edge passing through a small clutch of trees.

Continue ahead, when the gradient levels off, along a clear path to meet a major trail at a T-junction. Head right then left after 100 metres down a gentle slope to reach Brownlow Farm. Your approach might well set off a rabble-rousing chorus from geese, dogs and peacocks. It certainly did on my last visit. Make a sharp right through the farmyard to gain Crank Road.

Head left for 50 metres then fork off along a clear track on the opposite side of the road towards Beacon Wood. Halt at a gate and bear right along the edge of the wood until a kissing gate allows entry to the dense canopy overhead. A lack of adequate light within the wood has resulted in low level vegetation being eliminated to a large extent.

Pursue a direct course through the wood up an easy gradient heading due south. At the top end, you will emerge into the open air to pass through another kissing gate. Beyond this bear right through a thin stand of gorse. Another fence gate will find you approaching the squat edifice known as Billinge Beacon.

> *A rather sad and neglected monument, it deserves much more care than it has received to date. Superb views open out to the west across the rich farmland of West Lancashire. An ugly wire fence on the eastern lip surrounds the old quarry now used as a landfill site complete with scavenging seagulls. Dick Piers never saw the abrupt downfall in his frantic quest to escape the dreaded 'white rabbit'. A concrete trig column is barely noticed beside the fence. Once a favourite picnic spot, let us*

This squat edifice stands atop Billinge Hill.

hope that Billinge Beacon will soon be able to recapture the allure it once enjoyed.

Continue down a banking to enter a small cluster of gorse beyond which is a metal gate. Stroll down the passage to another gate after 100 metres, then swing right along a narrow path across a small field. After 100 metres bear left to merge with the access road serving the dumping ground. Walk down the road towards Billinge for a quarter mile before bearing right along an obvious track beside a hedge. Amble down the edge of the field to a road at the bottom.

Bear right past a number of exclusive stone residences to reach Red Barn Farm. The path swings left behind the farm buildings to continue

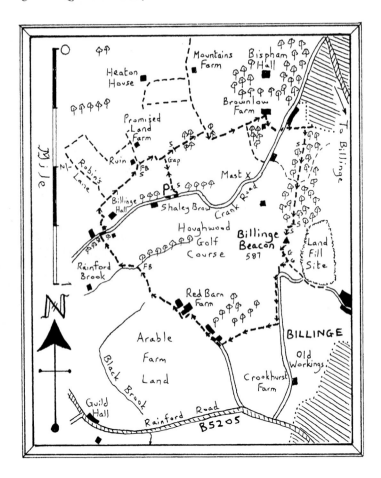

in a north-westerly direction towards Crank Road which we are informed on the signpost is exactly 0.82 kms distant. The path forges onward through fields that are likely to be chock full of wheat and peas by the summer to arrive at a footbridge spanning Black Brook.

Veer to the left along the edge of the next field bearing right away from the small stream after 150 metres to join Crank Road through a

An abandoned farm close to the 'promised land'.

line of trees. Bear right then left after 50 metres along a clear track that winds around to serve Promised Land Farm. The original owner obviously considered this area was his own personal nirvana. As you approach a left swing near to an old ruined farm, watch for the indistinct path leaning right through the adjoining hedge.

Straddle a footbridge and stile to follow the left side of the field uphill. On passing through the first gap swing a right alongside the fence to retrace your outward journey back to Crank Road.

TAKE IT ALL IN...
Read
Graham Dugdale's
walks FIRST in the
Lancaster Guardian
newspaper every Friday.
www.lancastertoday.co.uk